Journal & Devotional

Finding your kingly place of dominion in God

ANTHONIA UDEMEH

Copyright © 2023 Anthonia Udemeh

All rights reserved. No portion of this book may be reproduced in any form without written permission from the publisher or author.

ISBN: 978-1-7780878-3-7

Scripture quotations from The Holy Bible, New International Version® NIV® Copyright © 1973, 1978, 1984, 2011 by Biblica, Inc.
Used with permission. All rights reserved worldwide.

Scripture quotations marked (NLT) are taken from the Holy Bible, New Living Translation, copyright ©1996, 2004, 2015 by Tyndale House Foundation. Used by permission of Tyndale House Publishers, Carol Stream, Illinois 60188. All rights reserved.

Scripture quotations from The Authorized (King James) Version. Rights in the Authorized Version in the United Kingdom are vested in the Crown. Reproduced by permission of the Crown's patentee, Cambridge University Press.

Scripture quotations from The ESV® Bible (The Holy Bible, English Standard Version®), copyright © 2001 by Crossway, a publishing ministry of Good News Publishers. Used by permission. All rights reserved.

Book cover photography by Annie Spratt
Book cover design by Anthonia Udemeh

Dedication

This Journal & Devotional is dedicated to God and to all the women in the world who love God and desire to be more, and all that God has called them to be.

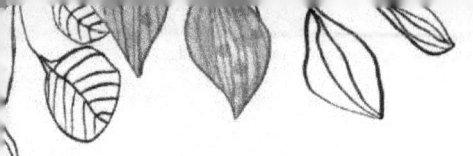

Contents

A letter to you i
Introduction ii
A Prayer of Salvation iv
Made for a purpose 1
You've got the power 3
Holy Spirit my helper 5
City set on a hill 7
My passion, my purpose 9
Fan the flame 11
Victory in the word 13
Washed in His blood 15
Christ is the rock 17
The rock is in me 19
All things through Christ 21
The void only God can fill 23
A tree of righteousness 25
Let the Spirit lead 27
Rest in the vine 29
Unashamed 31
Done with my past 33
Walk by faith 35
Redeemed 37
Justified 39
The Kingdom of God 41
The Fruit of the Spirit 43

Born to reign	45
The Kingdom is within you	47
Authority in Christ	49
Living sacrifice	51
Do things well	53
Lead from where you are	55
Lead by serving	57
Seek the Kingdom first	59
Do it afraid	61
Write the vision down	63
Start small	65
Don't stay small	67
Celebrate small wins	69
Get up and try again	71
Drink up	73
Learn something new	75
Make God's word a habit	77
Be wise	79
Find your voice	81
Thrive	83
Tares or wheat	85
No to slothfulness	87
Be a doer of the word	89
Work that is fireproof	91
We are the body	93
In deeds and in truth	95
Designed to multiply	97
The harvest is ready	99

This is eternal life	101
Go for gold, finish strong	103
Conclusion	105
Discover Your Purpose Trivia Quiz	106
Discover Your Purpose Trivia Quiz	107
Discover Your Purpose Trivia Quiz	108
Long-Term Vision Planner	109
Vision Planner – 6 months	110
Vision Planner – Year 1	111
Vision Planner – Year 2	112
Vision Planner – Year 3	113
Vision Planner – Year 4	114
Vision Planner – Year 5	115
Notes & Reflections	116
About the Author	123

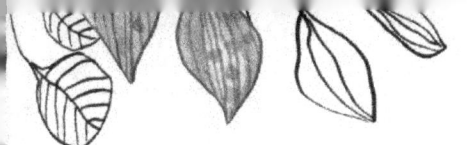

A letter to you

You are amazing! Yes, you. You are an amazing person, smart and beautiful. God created you with skills, talents, and abilities to become the best version of yourself.

Keep your head high, and shoulders squared because you are about to experience a mind-blowing encounter. I encourage you to write down your visions as you commit to your weekly goals using this journal to meditate on God's word.

Get Ready! Your life is about to be transformed!!!

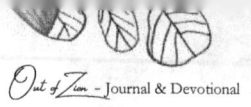

Introduction

I am a songwriter who enjoys writing. My best moments are spent with God and myself. Writing down as I hear God speak to me, writing down my thoughts, plans, visions, songs, and prayers. Writing helps me relieve stress, pour out my heart, memorize my plans and assess my progress.

I understand that the journey to finding one's purpose was never designed to be traveled alone; one could chase a thousand but two, ten thousand. For this reason, I made this journal and devotional to come along with you on this journey and help you become all that God wants you to be.

Out of Zion was an encounter I had in a vision where God showed me the end of time. God showed me the earth as He consumed it with His fire, but while the earth was consumed, God kept His children and brought us to a safe and peaceful place called Zion, where He dwells. And from that place came the song "Out of Zion".

I released the song, "Out of Zion", in November of 2022, but I knew God required more than just a song from this encounter. Understanding that we have come to Zion, the city of our God, to the place of His Kingdom, domain, and rulership is such a beautiful thing (Hebrews 12:22).

God, however, wants us to become more. God wants us to exercise our dominion on earth, which is why He created us to rule the earth, subdue it, and have dominion over it. God wants us to unleash His power within us on the earth even as we spread the message of Christ, which is the Kingdom of God, to the ends of the earth in every way.

Genesis 1:28 says: And God blessed them. And God said to them, "Be fruitful and multiply and fill the earth and subdue it and have dominion over the fish of the sea and the birds of the heavens and over every living thing that moves on the earth." Revelation 4:11 says: "You are worthy, our Lord and God, to receive glory and honor and power, for you created all things, and by your will, they were created and have their being."

These scriptures tell us that God desires that we have dominion and reign on the earth.

The essence of this journal and devotional is to help you find your purpose and place in God's Kingdom and through a conscious effort, get you started on your journey to becoming all that God wants you to be, and I want to come with you on this journey!

Throughout this journey and process of becoming, it is my prayer that you:
- Learn to know and hear God speak.
- Discover why God made you and what your purpose on earth is.
- Awaken your purpose and passion.
- Find your voice and place of dominion and authority.
- Overcome the obstacles preventing you from becoming all that God has made you to be.
- Take your place in God's Kingdom and begin to function in your royal authority as a daughter of Zion.
- Spread the gospel of God's Kingdom to the ends of the earth, so that God's glory will reign forever.

A Prayer of Salvation

Before I begin this Journey with you, I would love to invite you to God's amazing Kingdom if you haven't become a part of His Kingdom.

This book provides great insight into God's Kingdom, where He rules over us and gives us the power to rule over the earth. This power is available to all whom Jesus has become Lord over their lives, those whom He leads to eternal life.

If you would like to be a part of God's Kingdom, please pray this prayer with conviction in your heart:

"Dear God, I ask that you come into my heart and be my Lord and Saviour. I believe in my heart that Jesus Christ is God who came in the flesh to the earth, died for me, and was raised back to life from the dead, and I confess with my mouth that Jesus Christ is my Lord. I receive eternal life through God's Spirit that raised Jesus from the dead. I surrender to your Lordship as you rule over my heart and bring me to your Kingdom of light. Dear Lord, thank you because I am saved and born again into your Kingdom. In Jesus' name. Amen."

Welcome to God's Kingdom!

If you declare with your mouth, "Jesus is Lord," and believe in your heart that God raised Him from the dead, you will be saved - Romans 10:9 (NIV)

For it is by grace you have been saved, through faith - and this is not from yourselves, it is the gift of God - not by works, so that no one can boast. - Ephesians 2:8-9 (NIV)

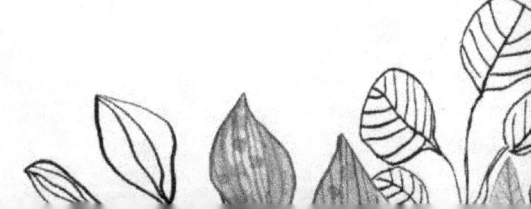

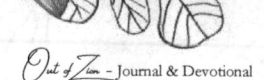

Week 1

Made for a purpose

For we are His workmanship, created in Christ Jesus unto good works, which God hath beforehand ordained, that we should walk in them.
Ephesians 2:10 (KJV)

Ephesians 2:10 tells us: He creates each of us by Christ Jesus to join Him in the work He does, this good work He has gotten ready for us to do. God made you for His pleasure (Revelation 4:11), to have dominion on the earth. And as you do, you please Him because you fulfill the reason why He made you.

We cannot fulfill our purpose of dominion outside of Christ. Christ is the King in this Kingdom, and He is the Kingdom of God. He brings us into Himself so that we can have dominion on the earth. In Christ, we can start our journey of becoming all we were created for. As heirs of God, co-heir with Christ (Romans 8:17), grafted into the vine, we are equipped with all we need to produce good works (2 Timothy 3:17).

We were made to function in Christ. We produce good works as heirs of the Kingdom through faith in His finished works. In the process, we rule and dominate the earth as we equip ourselves with the word of God.

*Date*_____

Question: What good works can you accomplish to help the spread of God's Kingdom on earth? What can you do to transform the world into a better place?

_____
_____
_____
_____
_____
_____
_____
_____
_____

Action: Write down three goals you will achieve this week to make the world a better place.

_____
_____
_____
_____
_____
_____
_____
_____

Prayer: Dear God, please reveal to me all the good works I was created to do on earth and assist me in getting started this week as I commit to pleasing you, in Jesus' name, Amen.

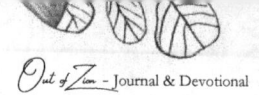

Week 2

You've got the power

For the Spirit God gave us does not make us timid, but gives us power, love, and self-discipline.
2 Timothy 1:7 (NIV)

For the Kingdom of God is not a matter of talk but of power (1 Corinthians 4:20). And by this divine power, He has given us everything we need for a godly life through our knowledge of Him who called us by His glory and goodness (1 Peter 1:3).

God has given us the gift of His Holy Spirit, which is the Spirit of boldness and confidence, not timidity. The Holy Spirit empowers us and gives us the courage to achieve greatness. As we believe in Christ, we receive this Spirit, so we can practice our faith, and act boldly and confidently in every area of our lives and in everything we do, whether at work, school, home, or business. This Spirit of boldness that comes from our confidence in God is what God wants us to show forth. We demonstrate the power of God within us as we act in boldness and without fear or intimidation, for our God is the Lion of the tribe of Judah. You have that boldness within you. Why not let it out?

We express this power within us when we begin to act courageously in faith rather than fear, allowing us to reign, dominate, and lead this godly life God has called us to. When we do this, we begin to live out the gospel, which leads to even more fruit in God's Kingdom.

Date _____

Question: What makes you afraid? Write down your fears.

_____
_____
_____
_____
_____
_____
_____
_____
_____
_____
_____
_____

Action: Write down three actions you will take this week to overcome your fears.

_____
_____
_____
_____
_____
_____
_____
_____
_____
_____

Prayer: Dear God, I pray that out of your glorious riches, you will strengthen me with the power through your Holy Spirit in my inner being to unleash boldness and confidence in all I do this week. In Jesus' name, Amen.

Week 3

Holy Spirit my helper

But the Advocate, the Holy Spirit, whom the Father will send in my name, will teach you all things and will remind you of everything I have said to you.
John 14:26 (NIV)

Sometimes, trying to achieve the goals we set for ourselves might seem daunting or unachievable. We tend to beat ourselves too hard, get frustrated, or throw in the towel when things don't go as planned.

"Don't try to achieve your goals all by yourself." That's what God is saying to you now. Remember that the goals you've set out to accomplish so far in this journal have been inspired by God, so you must lean on Him to help you achieve them, for without Christ, you can do nothing (John 15:5). Rely on the Holy Spirit for everything and don't be afraid or too shy to ask for help, even for the simplest things. If you fall short or fail, get back up and try again. Don't stay down for too long. When you pray to God for help, the Holy Spirit will come through for you.

As you strive with the help of God to achieve your set goals, go at the pace that works for you. Keep your focus on your goals, and don't get distracted by what others might or might not be doing. Remember that your assignment and purpose are unique to you. So don't try to compete with anyone else but yourself.

*Date*_____

Question: In what areas, and with what do you need the help of the Holy Spirit in your life?

_____
_____
_____
_____
_____
_____
_____
_____
_____
_____
_____

Action: Write down 3 things you want the Holy Spirit to help you with as it pertains to achieving your goals.

_____
_____
_____
_____
_____
_____
_____

Prayer: Dear Holy Spirit, I need your help in these areas (mention them). Please teach me and remind me of God's word and empower me to have faith, and to believe I can do all things through Christ.
In Jesus' name, Amen.

Week 4

City set on a hill

You are the light of the world. A city that is set on a hill cannot be hidden.
Matthew 5:14 (KJV)

Christ came as the light of the world, so as we receive Him into our hearts and allow the light of God's word to shine in our hearts, we become the light. You are the light of the world. This means the world is in darkness and needs you to shine your light.

What then is light? Light is God and everything God represents. 1 John 1:5 says, "This is the message we have heard from Him and announce to you, that God is light, and in Him, there is no darkness at all." As believers and followers of Jesus Christ, we are God's representatives here on earth. God expects us to shine the light He has put in us to the world. Jesus said in Matthew 5:16, "Let your light so shine before men, that they may see your good works and glorify your Father in heaven." You were born to shine, so shine!!!

You start to shine when you allow God in you to gain expression through the things you do and the way you live your life. Is there something God has placed in your heart to do? A skill, or talent, at work, school, or business? Do it well, do it like God wants you to, and do it to please God. This is how you shine your light and glorify God.

Date_____

Question: What special skills and talents do you have? Write them down.

_____
_____
_____
_____
_____
_____
_____
_____
_____
_____
_____

Action: Write down 3 ways you can use your skills and talents this week.

_____
_____
_____
_____
_____
_____
_____

Prayer: Dear Father, thank you for making me the light of the world. I recognize that I am your representative here on earth. Reveal to me this light you have put in me and show me how to shine your light. In Jesus' name, Amen.

Week 5

My passion, my purpose

For God is working in you, giving you the desire and the power to do what pleases Him.
Philippians 2:13 (NLT)

As we come into God's Kingdom, through the understanding of the message of Christ, God redesigns our passions and desires to align with His purpose. We find our desires and priorities changing, realigning with God's plans for our lives. This is the working power of God in us, giving us the desire and ability to do what pleases Him. This power is so strong that you find a war within you when you do not do the things that please God. This is because you have become a different person. One with the Spirit of God that desires only to please God (2 Corinthians 5:17).

Now that you have desired and made Christ your Lord and have believed in your heart that He is God who died and resurrected, you are now a part of God's Kingdom. Your talents, skills, and ability must align with your new desires to please God. This is how you can begin the work of the Kingdom and start living out the purpose which God created you for. You should direct your passion toward God and humanity. Aligning your talents, skills, and abilities with God and humanity is fulfilling your purpose.

Making a deliberate and consistent effort towards serving God and humanity with your gifts and talents is how you fulfill your purpose and take your place in God's Kingdom.

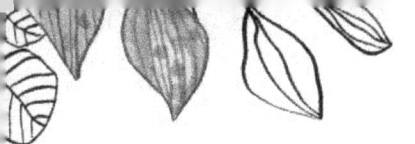

Out of Zion – Journal & Devotional

*Date*_____

Question: What is that new passion you received when you were born again? A passion for God and for what specific people or things?

_____
_____
_____
_____
_____
_____
_____
_____
_____
_____
_____
_____

Action: Write down 3 ways you can redirect your skills and talents toward pleasing God and loving people.

_____
_____
_____
_____
_____
_____
_____
_____
_____
_____

Prayer: Dear Father, show me how to love people and please you. Reveal to me how I can use my skills, talents, and abilities to serve humanity and please you. In Jesus' name, Amen.

Week 6

Fan the flame

For this reason, I remind you to fan into flame the gift of God, which is in you through the laying on of my hands.
2 Timothy 1:6 (NIV)

You have the gift of God in you. It could be a tiny spark that God expects us to fan into flame. 1 Peter 4:10 tells us, "As each one has received a special gift, employ it in serving one another as good stewards of the manifold grace of God." This is one way to fan into flame this special gift of God.

It's also important for us to be aware of the gift of God in us so we can begin to fan it into flame. It starts from the place of prayer and knowing some of these gifts of God.

According to 1 Corinthians 12:8 – 10, these are the foundational gifts of God on which we build on:
1) The gift of wisdom.
2) The gift of knowledge
3) The gift of faith
4) The gift of healing
5) The gift of miraculous powers
6) The gift of prophecy
7) The gift of discernment of spirits
8) The gift of speaking in different kinds of tongues
9) The gift of interpretation of tongues

Date_____

Question: As you read through the gifts listed on the previous page, write down the gifts your heart is drawn towards.

_____
_____
_____
_____
_____
_____
_____
_____
_____
_____
_____
_____

Action: In accordance with 1 Peter 4:10, write down 3 ways you can use these gifts you have identified in serving people.

_____
_____
_____
_____
_____
_____
_____

Prayer: Dear God, reveal to me all the gifts you have put in me, and as I have desired these gifts (mention them), grant them to me and teach me how to use them in serving you and humanity. In Jesus' name, Amen.

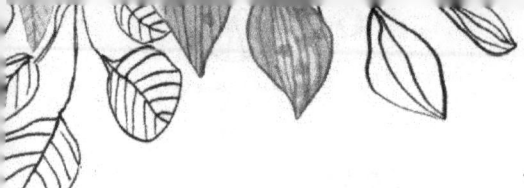

Week 7

Victory in the word

For everyone who has been born of God overcomes the world. And this is the victory that has overcome the world—our faith
1 John 5:4 (ESV)

Our faith in Christ and His word gives us victory over the lies of the enemy, whose words are contrary to the words of Christ. And as we believe the words of Christ, we speak them into being (2 Corinthians 4:13). In doing this, we fight the good fight of faith and receive victory and the crown of righteousness (2 Timothy 4: 7-8).

It is this victory that empowers us with authority and power in the Kingdom of God, where we can govern the earth, rule, and have dominion.

We may experience obstacles and challenges when trying to put our skills and talents to work on earth to serve God and humanity. This battlefield is in our minds, and we must renew our minds (Romans 12:2) and tear down every argument that opposes us with the word of God (2 Corinthians 10:5). So, when there's a voice in your head that tells you that you are not good enough, or that you are a failure or a nobody, take on the full armor of God (Ephesians 6:13) and speak the word of God to counter that lie of the enemy. This is how you gain victory, claim your ruling seat in the Kingdom of God, and begin to dominate the earth.

 Journal & Devotional

Date_____

Question: What are some of the negative thoughts you think towards yourself?

_____
_____
_____
_____
_____
_____
_____
_____
_____
_____

Action: Write down the positive of those negative words according to what God says about you.

_____
_____
_____
_____
_____
_____
_____
_____
_____
_____

Prayer: Throughout this week God, I choose to speak your word of life into existence. I ask that you reveal and remove any negativity and obstacle in my life that hinder me from manifesting my gifts and talents. In Jesus' name, Amen.

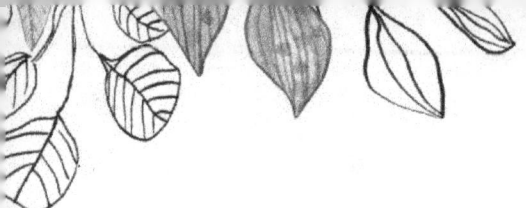

Week 8

Washed in His blood

And so, dear brothers and sisters, we can boldly enter heaven's Most Holy Place because of the blood of Jesus.
Hebrews 10:19 (NLT)

As people who once struggled with sin and guilt, we sometimes experience impostor syndrome, the feeling that we are incompetent and unqualified for the position we now have in God's Kingdom, and we must overcome this imposter syndrome to operate in our new position in Christ.

Hebrews 10: 20 – 22 says, "By His death, Jesus opened a new and life-giving way through the curtain into the Most Holy Place. And since we have a great High Priest who rules over God's house, let us go right into the presence of God with sincere hearts fully trusting Him. For our guilty consciences have been sprinkled with Christ's blood to make us clean, and our bodies have been washed with pure water."

For us to operate in God's Kingdom and have dominion on the earth, we must believe that Christ died for us, and His blood gives us the full privilege to function in the Kingdom of God. You have become a priest unto God and must get rid of the guilt of sin and condemnation because Christ has paid the price for your sin and has set you free!!!

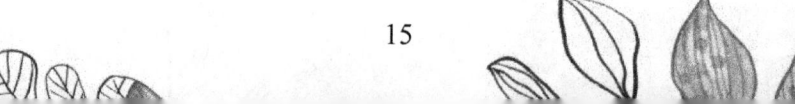

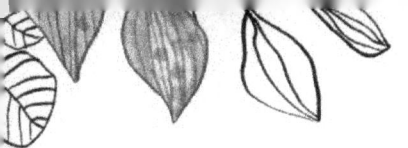 

Date_____

Question: In what ways do you feel unqualified to be in the presence of God?

_____
_____
_____
_____
_____
_____
_____
_____
_____
_____
_____
_____

Action: Write down Hebrews 10:20-22 but personalize it and include your name in the statement.

_____
_____
_____
_____
_____
_____
_____
_____
_____
_____
_____

Prayer: Dear God, thank you because I have the full privilege to function in your Kingdom and I no longer feel unqualified because Christ sets me free. Pray your personalized Hebrews 10:20-22 statement.

Week 9

Christ is the rock

Behold, I am the one who has laid as a foundation in Zion, a stone, a tested stone, a precious cornerstone, of a sure foundation: 'Whoever believes will not be in haste.'
Isaiah 28:16 (ESV)

Christ is the rock who came to lay down His life as the foundation and chief cornerstone in establishing God's Kingdom here on earth. 1 Corinthians 3:11 tells us, "For no other foundation can anyone lay than that which is laid, which is Jesus Christ."

As we assume our position in God's Kingdom and begin to build on Christ's foundation by using our abilities and talents to spread the message of Christ, serve mankind, and please God, we must ensure that we are building on Christ. We must ensure we are acting in line with the words of Christ, obeying His words as He has commanded. This is how we can ensure our work on earth is forever lasting.

Jesus said in Luke 6:47-49, "Whoever comes to Me, and hears My sayings and does them, I will show you whom he is like: He is like a man building a house, who dug deep and laid the foundation on the rock. And when the flood arose, the stream beat vehemently against that house, and could not shake it, for it was founded on the rock. But he who heard and did nothing is like a man who built a house on the earth without a foundation, against which the stream beat vehemently; and immediately it fell. And the ruin of that house was great."

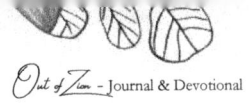

Date_____

Question: Read any of the parables from the book of Matthew. What teachings of Christ can you apply as you begin to put your talent to work?

_____
_____
_____
_____
_____
_____
_____
_____
_____
_____
_____

Action: Write down 3 ways you can lead an exemplary Christ-like life this week.

_____
_____
_____
_____
_____
_____
_____
_____
_____

Prayer: Dear God, help me to be like Christ in every way and every day. Teach me how to build on this foundation of Christ and take the message of Christ to the ends of the earth. In Jesus' name, Amen.

Week 10

The rock is in me

Whoever believes in me, as Scripture has said, rivers of living water will flow from within them.
John 7:38 (NIV)

We drink of Christ, this rock, in the place of fellowship and communion with Christ, by studying the word of God, meditating on it, and praying it. As we do, we fill ourselves up with God's words, and Christ who is the rock gets formed in us (Galatians 4:19). This Christ is the Kingdom of God within us (Luke 17:21) and becomes the chief cornerstone which is laid as a foundation in us by which we must build on.

As we build, by acting in obedience to God's words and instructions, this rock in us gains expression, and we become a fountain of living water from which others come to draw from. This is how we become the light of the world and begin to dominate and rule.

Isaiah 60 speaks of the glory of Zion, which comes when we believe in Christ, who is our rock, and stand on Him as a firm foundation. We emit the light of Christ, which is in us to the world, and the river of living water flowing from the rock in us is released on the earth to serve our world.

We rule, dominate the earth and build this Kingdom of God on the earth together with Christ as co-laborers (1 Corinthians 3:19), when we have Christ the rock in us!!!

*Date*_____

Question: Read a chapter from the book of Mark. What teachings of Christ can you allow to get formed in you?

_____
_____
_____
_____
_____
_____
_____
_____
_____
_____
_____

Action: Write down 3 ways you can allow Christ to express Himself through you this week.

_____
_____
_____
_____
_____
_____
_____
_____

Prayer: Dear Jesus, I ask that you come and be formed in me. Let your teachings take root in me until you become a rock inside of me that can gush out living water to serve my purpose in your Kingdom. In Jesus' name, Amen.

Week 11

All things through Christ

I can do all this through Him who gives me strength.
Philippians 4:13 (NIV)

As we write down our plans and visions, sometimes they might seem so big and daunting, almost impossible to achieve, but the bible tells us that we can do all things through Christ because He strengthens us for our unique purpose and assignment. The moment we believe this, we open our minds to seeing ways by which we can accomplish them. When we believe we can achieve anything in Christ, we begin to experience divine breakthroughs working it out for our good.

Hebrews 12:1 tells us that we are surrounded by a huge crowd of witnesses who have lived the faith and is cheering us up and telling us we can do this. Let us strip off every weight that slows us down, especially the sin (of unbelief) that so easily trips us up. And let us run with endurance the race God has set before us by keeping our eyes on Jesus, the champion who initiates and perfects our faith to believe we can do this because He is in us, and we are in Him!

If you ever doubt your ability to dominate and rule on the earth, let the message in Hebrews 12 encourage you. God believes in you, and that's why He gave you the assignment to have dominion on the earth. Now you must believe in yourself against any reasonable doubt. You've got this, you can do this. Go ahead and have dominion!!!

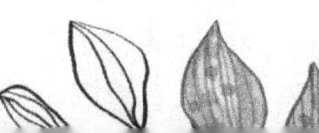

*Date*_____

Question: What are your dreams, and what seems impossible when you try to achieve them?

_____
_____
_____
_____
_____
_____
_____
_____
_____
_____
_____
_____

Action: Write down 3 actions you can take this week to lead you closer to achieving your plans.

_____
_____
_____
_____
_____
_____
_____
_____

Prayer: Dear God, thank you for the vision you have given me. Thank you because I can achieve them through Christ. Help me to see ways in which I can start achieving my dreams. In Jesus' name, Amen.

Week 12

The void only God can fill

He has made everything beautiful in its time. He has also set eternity in the human heart, yet no one can fathom what God has done from beginning to end.
Ecclesiastes 3:11 (NIV)

Human needs are insatiable, leading to a constant desire to acquire, achieve, and become more. For this reason, we need to set our priorities right, so we don't chase after temporal yet insatiable things, or make ourselves a god.

In the end, God will shake the earth and remove everything that can be shaken, leaving only those things that are eternal in the Kingdom of God which cannot be shaken, those things that have been built on Christ the firm foundation (Hebrews 12: 26-29).

We must allow God to be the motive behind all we do. He must be the reason why we do the things we do (Colossians 3:23). As you set your goals and priorities, write down your visions, have the eternal Kingdom of God in mind, with your focus on being like Christ and spreading the message of Christ to the ends of the earth.

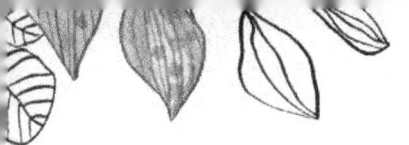

Date_____

Question: How do your plans, dreams, and visions reflect Christ and the message of Christ which is the Kingdom of God?

_____
_____
_____
_____
_____
_____
_____
_____
_____
_____
_____

Action: Write down 3 ways you can spread the message of Christ or be like Christ this week.

_____
_____
_____
_____
_____
_____
_____
_____
_____

Prayer: Dear God, thank you for showing me that only you can truly satisfy me. Help me to make you my priority and the reason why I do all the things that I do.
In Jesus' name, Amen.

Week 13

A tree of righteousness

To appoint unto them that mourn in Zion, to give unto them beauty for ashes, the oil of joy for mourning, the garment of praise for the spirit of heaviness; that they might be called trees of righteousness, the planting of the Lord, that He might be glorified.
Isaiah 61:3 (KJV)

Isaiah 60 – 61 speaks of what would happen at the appearance of our light which is Christ, the light of the world. When Christ gets revealed to us, as we receive light by the knowledge of God through the understanding of Christ's message, we become like Christ, transformed into His image (2 Corinthians 3:18). We are also made to become a tree of righteousness, grafted into the righteous vine – Jesus.

This transformation becomes our new identity in God's Kingdom. It is this identity that gives us the right into the Kingdom of God to rule and reign with Christ (John 1:12-15). As we live our lives here on earth, we must live in the consciousness of who we are – a tree of righteousness with branches that flourish, bearing the fruit of the Spirit.

Living with this consciousness of right standing with God is how we can effectively function in the Kingdom of God, with full faith and confidence to do the work of the Kingdom as Christ's ambassadors on the earth, bringing the Kingdom of God to the earth (John 10:9).

Date_____

Question: How does your new identity as the righteousness of God help you function on the earth as Christ's ambassador?

_____
_____
_____
_____
_____
_____
_____
_____
_____
_____
_____

Action: In 3 sentences, explain how your new identity makes you feel.

_____
_____
_____
_____
_____
_____
_____
_____
_____

Prayer: Dear God, thank you for making me a tree of righteousness. I receive this new identity with gladness of heart, knowing that I have full access to function in your Kingdom. In Jesus' name, Amen.

Week 14

Let the Spirit lead

All who are led by the Spirit of God are sons of God.
Romans 8:14 (ESV)

The Holy Spirit in us leads us daily through the word of God. God speaks in diverse ways, and the Spirit of God helps us identify God's voice by bearing witness with our spirit (Romans 8:16). The Holy Spirit's guidance is important in our walk with God. When we consistently submit ourselves to the voice of the Holy Spirit, we give the Holy Spirit more permission to lead us.

In God's Kingdom, obedience is an essential aspect of reigning. The Holy Spirit may sometimes lead us to unexpected places, but our reaction in obedience because we believe and trust God's voice, will bring glory to God. The Holy Spirit led Jesus to the wilderness to be tempted; He led Ezekiel to the valley of dry bones and Phillip to the desert, but they were all to reveal God's glory (Acts 8:26, Ezekiel 37:1, Matthew 4:1).

Our experiences in life, both good and bad, all work together to bring God glory even as they direct us to the place of our purpose and calling. As we go through life, tests and trials are necessary to build our faith and make us all we were called to be. Even Jesus was tested in the wilderness, and His obedience to die on the cross brought us salvation (Philippians 2:8). Likewise, we also must yield to the Spirit of God, that voice of peace that leads us to become more like God, and all that God wants us to be.

 *Out of Zion* - Journal & Devotional

Date_____

Question: What has the Holy Spirit been nudging you to do lately? The voice of peace that speaks to your heart to do what is pleasing to God is the voice of the Holy Spirit.

_____
_____
_____
_____
_____
_____
_____
_____
_____

Action: Write down 3 things you will do this week as you let the Holy Spirit lead you.

_____
_____
_____
_____
_____
_____
_____

Prayer: Heavenly Father, thank you for your Holy Spirit in me that speaks peace and righteousness to my heart. Help me to yield myself to the voice of your Spirit always.
In Jesus' name, Amen.

Week 15

Rest in the vine

Remain in me, as I also remain in you. No branch can bear fruit by itself; it must remain in the vine. Neither can you bear fruit unless you remain in me?
John 15:4 (NIV)

We have become the body of Christ, and John 15:4 describes us as a branch of Christ. As we all know, branches cannot survive outside of the tree, and neither can they bear fruit. In the same way, we cannot function in the Kingdom of God unless we stay grafted in the vine.

How do we stay grafted in the vine – Christ? We must commit to seeking Him, which includes desiring to do the Kingdom's will. But this is the first part of what's required. The second part is in letting the word of God in our hearts bear fruit (John 15:7). These two combined give us the keys of the Kingdom, our dominion, and authority, where we can ask whatsoever, we will (because our will and desires are in line with the Kingdom's will), and it will be done.

The rights we have into the Kingdom of God are through Christ's blood, that sacrifice He offered on the cross. Our rulership and dominion come when we start allowing the words of Christ to take root in us as we commit to following Christ and obeying His word.

*Date*_____

Question: What aspect of Christ's teachings do you find difficult to follow and obey?

_____
_____
_____
_____
_____
_____
_____
_____
_____
_____
_____

Action: Write down 3 ways you can deliberately start obeying the voice of God which you hear in His word.

_____
_____
_____
_____
_____
_____
_____
_____
_____

Prayer: Dear God, thank you for making me your branch and for grafting me into the vine, Jesus Christ. I commit to following Christ and obeying Him even as I let His word into my heart. I receive the keys of the Kingdom.
In Jesus' name, Amen.

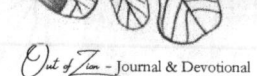

Week 16

Unashamed

For I am not ashamed of this Good News about Christ. It is the power of God at work, saving everyone who believes—the Jew first and also the Gentile.
Romans 1:16 (NLT)

As believers and followers of Christ, God wants us to spread the His word to the ends of the earth. This is what it means to operate in the Kingdom of God. How can we carry the message of Christ throughout the earth? The simple answer is by living the word. We must become so interwoven in His word that it makes up our DNA and who we are.

Surrendering yourself in obedience to God and the instruction of the Holy Spirit is how you can start. So, you might ask, how do I know when the Holy Spirit is instructing me on something? The voice of God brings peace, and when you follow that voice, you experience the fruit of the Spirit (Galatians 5:23)

If we want to function in our kingly position as daughters of Zion, we must not be ashamed of the Kingdom we represent. We must not be afraid of becoming all that Christ is. We must not be ashamed to come before Him bearing our hearts out and we must not be afraid to let Him undo us, remold us, work in us and transform us into His very own self.

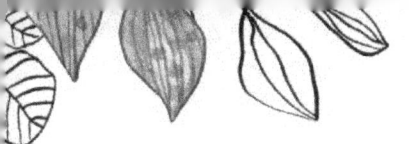 

*Date*_____

Question: Do you feel ashamed about spreading the message of Christ? Write down how you feel about spreading the message of Christ.

_____
_____
_____
_____
_____
_____
_____
_____
_____
_____

Action: Write down 3 ways you can spread the message of Christ this week.

_____
_____
_____
_____
_____
_____
_____
_____

Prayer: Heavenly Father, thank you for your Son, Jesus Christ, who despised the shame just to save me. Help me to be unashamed of the gospel of Christ in every way, just as Christ was unashamed to go to the cross for me.
In Jesus' name, Amen.

Week 17

Done with my past

Therefore, if anyone is in Christ, he is a new creation. The old has passed away; behold, the new has come
2 Corinthian 5:17 (ESV)

Our past was gone when we entered that door – Christ. Our old self was left behind, and we were made a new creation. Now, we must forget the past and press toward the mark for the prize of a higher calling of God in Christ Jesus (Philippians 3:14). Press on so that you may attain perfection through Christ.

Yes, Christ wants us to attain a perfection that comes from us beholding His face as we read His word and become transformed daily into His perfect image from glory to glory (2 Corinthians 3:18). For this reason, we must let Christ finish His work in us as we give Him just a little more room in our lives daily.

Following Jesus requires us to leave our past (our old self) behind and take on this new identity where we have become the righteousness of God in Christ and trust the words of Christ and all He says you are. This allows us to experience the transformation that comes from seeing the face of Christ. Remember that you serve as Christ in this Kingdom and can only exercise dominion on earth when you become like Christ.

Out of Zion - Journal & Devotional

Date_____

Question: What sins of the past hold you back and make you feel a sense of guilt, shame, or fear?

_____
_____
_____
_____
_____
_____
_____
_____

Action: Write down 3 things about your past you'll like to forget and next to them, write down your new identity in Christ that replaces your old identity.

_____
_____
_____
_____
_____
_____
_____
_____
_____

Prayer: Dear God, thank you for the new identity I have now in Christ. Thank you for transforming me to be like Christ. Now I can function in your Kingdom because I function as Christ who has become my new identity. In Jesus' name, Amen.

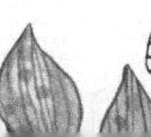

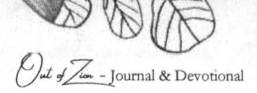

Week 18

Walk by faith

For we live by faith, not by sight.
2 Corinthians 5:7 (ESV)

We have a new life in Christ, and the first step to living this new royal life is to truly believe that you are chosen for this purpose. Faith is the currency transacted in this Kingdom, which is how everything works. You cannot enjoy life or begin to exercise dominion until you believe you are royalty and have become part of the Kingdom of God.

You believe first and then you see (John 11:40). A mustard seed faith is all you need to have dominion and rule over the earth (Mark 4:30-32). The mustard seed faith has potent power, the same power that can raise the dead and work mighty miracles. But we must start by planting our mustard seed faith by doing the little things in the Kingdom, and as we do, we grow to occupy even greater roles and take on greater responsibilities (1 Peter 2:2).

Jesus told a parable of the talent to illustrate what the Kingdom of God is about. The servants that multiplied their talents were given more, and the one that did not multiply but rather buried his talent was taken out of the Kingdom, and his talent was given to the multipliers. It takes faith to multiply your gifts and talents as you function in the Kingdom of God. Let your light shine and give God the glory, He will multiply you because you walked by faith (Matthew 25:14-30).

 *Out of Zion* - Journal & Devotional

Date_____

Question: What has God said about you in His word that you struggle to believe?

_____
_____
_____
_____
_____
_____
_____
_____
_____
_____
_____

Action: Write down 3 things you will start doing in faith to put your gift and talent to work, even when you are unsure it would yield any fruit.

_____
_____
_____
_____
_____
_____
_____

Prayer: Thank you God for who I am in Christ. I believe I am part of your Kingdom, and I am royalty. I receive faith to put my gifts and talents to work in this Kingdom that I am a part of. In Jesus' name, Amen.

Week 19

Redeemed

Zion shall be redeemed by justice and those in her who repent, by righteousness.
Isaiah 1:27 (ESV)

You have been redeemed and restored to Zion, God's Kingdom, because of what Christ did on the cross, which grants you a righteous status. This is the status that permits us to function in God's Kingdom.

As people who have been set free, we must intentionally walk in this freedom, understanding that our status as royalty in Zion is not based on the tasks we accomplish, but on our confidence in Christ. We don't do the work of God to make it to heaven only. Rather, we have been brought to the Kingdom of God because we believe in what Christ did for us at the cross, and this compels us to do the things we do because we love God (1 John 4:19).

Walk in this consciousness that you are redeemed, set free, delivered, and restored to Zion. Here at Zion, you have received a royal office where you should function. You function by putting your skills and talent to work to spread the message of Christ, which is the Kingdom of God, to the ends of the earth. God has hired you to function as royalty in this Kingdom. Now it's time to take on that royal responsibility to rule and reign on the earth.

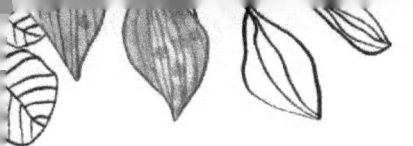
 Out of Zion - Journal & Devotional

Date_____

Question: In what ways can you begin to function in your royal office at Zion? Consider ways you can put your skills and talents to work in spreading the message of Christ.

_____
_____
_____
_____
_____
_____
_____
_____
_____
_____
_____

Action: Write down 3 things you will start doing to spread the message of Christ this week.

_____
_____
_____
_____
_____
_____
_____

Prayer: Thank you God for my royal office at Zion where I function as the righteousness of God in Christ. Help me to put my skills and talent to work in this office to spread the message of Christ. In Jesus' name, Amen.

Week 20

Justified

So now there is no condemnation for those who belong to Christ Jesus.
Romans 8:1 (NLT)

Do you ever feel weighed down by sin, preventing you from worshiping, praying, meditating, or reading God's word? Do you become reminded of what you did last summer or last night every time you come into God's presence? That is the voice of the accuser, which you must silence.

To function in this Kingdom, we must always put on the full armor of God in preparation to demolish any weapon of the enemy plotted to make us unfruitful in the Kingdom. Ephesians 6:10-18 tells us about the armor of God:
· The belt of truth
· Breastplate of righteousness
· Shield of faith
· Helmet of salvation
· Sword of the spirit, which is the word of God
Praying always and being always ready to spread the gospel of peace. In other words, having the zeal to function in the Kingdom of God and spread the message of Christ.

Doing this makes us defeat the enemy that brings accusations and condemnation to stop us from functioning in the Kingdom.

Date_____

Question: Do you feel condemned or unworthy to come before God when you try to pray, worship, or study His word? Write down what you feel condemned about.

_____
_____
_____
_____
_____
_____
_____
_____
_____
_____

Action: Christ's sacrifice on the cross makes you justified. Act in faith now and write to God about anything on your mind because you have been set free.

_____
_____
_____
_____
_____
_____
_____
_____
_____
_____

Prayer: Thank you God because I have been set free and I am not condemned because Christ has paid the sacrifice for my sins on the cross. I am free. In Jesus' name, Amen.

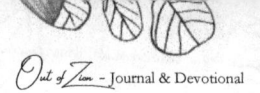

Week 21

The Kingdom of God

He told them another parable: "The Kingdom of heaven is like a mustard seed, which a man took and planted in his field. Though it is the smallest of all seeds, yet when it grows, it is the largest of garden plants and becomes a tree, so that the birds come and perch in its branches."
Matthew 13:31-32 (NIV)

The Kingdom of God is the word of God. It is like a seed planted that grows and multiplies. It is a treasure we find in Christ and as we get planted in the word and allow the word, which is Christ, to take root in us, we begin to grow (Matthew 13:31, John 15:4). God wants us to bear fruit in this Kingdom and become disciples of the Kingdom.

You are a disciple of the Kingdom when you allow the seed of God's word to take root in your heart. As you believe the word, you begin to bear fruits, and these fruits become treasures within you that you can bring forth into the world (Matthew 13:44). This is what having dominion in the Kingdom is all about (Matthew 13:51).

God plants His word in our hearts so we can bear fruits and grow to serve generations. The treasures within us, which are God's word, our gifts, and our talents were given to us to serve humanity and we should direct them toward expanding the gospel and message of Jesus Christ.

Date_____

Question: What word has God planted in your heart that has taken root in you? What word have you come to believe and hold as truth with evidence? Share your testimony.

_____
_____
_____
_____
_____
_____
_____
_____
_____
_____
_____
_____

Action: Write down 3 ways you can spread that word to inspire faith in others this week.

_____
_____
_____
_____
_____
_____
_____
_____

Prayer: Dear God, thank you for planting your word in my heart and giving me the water of life to grow your word in me. Help me to share this with others around me to help increase their faith in you. In Jesus' name, Amen.

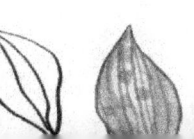

Week 22

The Fruit of the Spirit

> But the Holy Spirit produces this kind of fruit in our lives: love, joy, peace, patience, kindness, goodness, faithfulness, gentleness, and self-control. There is no law against these.
> *Galatians 5:22-23 (NLT)*

The Spirit of God is the nature and force of God within us that we received when we became born again. This nature and force of God is the power of God within us to have dominion on the earth. As we allow God's word to be planted in our hearts by faith, we receive the Holy Spirit, who gains expression through us. These expressions are seen as the fruit of the spirit. It changes our DNA to that of God.

The lifestyle and culture within God's Kingdom are very different from what we see outside of the Kingdom in the world. As ambassadors and citizens of the Kingdom of God, we must make positive impacts in the world through the fruit we bear. This is how we shine our light and take our place in the Kingdom. In so doing, we bear more fruit (John 15:2, Matthew 5:16-18).

This fruit that the Holy Spirit bears in us is the evidence of our faith and becomes the seed that can be planted in others to inspire them to embrace God's character through faith. Living in the Kingdom of God entails expressing the fruit of the Holy Spirit, which is, love, kindness, joy, peace, patience, goodness, faithfulness, gentleness, and self-control. We rule and reign on the earth as bear this fruit.

Date_____

Question: What fruit of the Spirit do you have, and which do you need to grow? Reading, meditating, and praying God's word allows the Holy Spirit to bear more fruit in you.

The Fruit of the Spirit in me	The Fruit of the Spirit that needs to grow more in me

Action: Write down 3 ways you can give the fruit of the Spirit to people around you this week.

_____
_____
_____
_____
_____
_____
_____
_____

Prayer: Thank you God for your nature and power in me, in the person of the Holy Spirit. I yield myself to your Spirit so you can bear fruit in me. In Jesus' name, Amen.

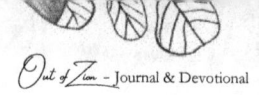

Week 23

Born to reign

You have made them to be a Kingdom and priests to serve our God, and they will reign on the earth."
Revelation 5:10 (NIV)

The believers of Jesus Christ make up the Kingdom of God and serve as priests unto God. A priest is a person who serves as a mediator between a people and their God. Christ is our high priest that offered Himself as a sacrifice to reconcile the world back to God. He came on the earth to establish this Kingdom of God, setting Himself as the chief cornerstone and laying his life as a foundation for the continuity of the work of the Kingdom.

He then made us priests unto God in this Kingdom and gave us the ministry of reconciliation (2 Corinthians 5:18). Passing the torch to us to keep on spreading this gospel. He is still working together with us in fulfilling the great commission of going into the world to make disciples of the Kingdom, just as we have become one of His.

What this means is that we must serve as priests under the leadership and authority of the high priest who came to show us the way to live – meaning the way to function in the Kingdom. You were born to reign under the authority of Christ. Reign in love, reign over every negativity. Let Christ be formed in you so you can be Christ in the flesh here on the earth. This is your place in the Kingdom.

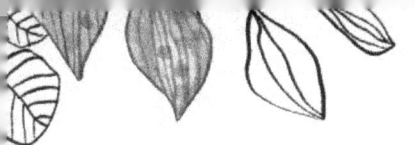

Date_____

Question: What word has God planted in your heart that inspires you to share with others?

_____
_____
_____
_____
_____
_____
_____
_____
_____
_____

Action: Write down 3 ways you can serve as a priest and bring people closer to God

_____
_____
_____
_____
_____
_____
_____
_____

Prayer: Heavenly Father, thank you for planting your word in my heart and inspiring me to serve in your Kingdom. Help me to share this with others around me even as I take on my priestly position in your Kingdom. In Jesus' name, Amen.

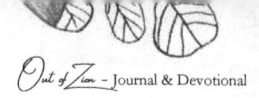

Week 24

The Kingdom is within you

Neither shall they say, Lo here! or, lo there! for, behold, the Kingdom of God is within you.
Luke 17:21(KJV)

As the body of Christ, we have become the temple of the living God (1 Corinthians 6:19-20). Acts 7:48-49 tells us that God does not live in temples made by human hands for heaven is His throne and the earth His footstool. We are the resting place for God's feet, walking the earth to spread the message of the Kingdom. To function in the Kingdom, we must live in Christ, move and have our being in Him.

The Kingdom of God is Christ gaining expression on the earth through the workings of the Holy Spirit in every believer. So that we cannot enter the Kingdom of God unless we are born of water (with minds renewed by the word of God) and of the Spirit (with hearts opened to receiving the Holy Spirit, letting Him have expressions through you and bear fruit in you) (John 3:5).

Jesus Christ and the Holy Spirit give us access to the Kingdom of God and empower us to function in our office in God's Kingdom. It is that power within us that compels us to do the will of God; to reign and have dominion. God's Kingdom has been established in the person of Jesus Christ who lives in you. Now go about planting that same Kingdom you have received into the hearts of people around you.

Date_____

Question: What aspect of the Kingdom of God (the message of Christ) has been established in your heart that you can give expression to?

_____
_____
_____
_____
_____
_____
_____
_____
_____
_____
_____
_____

Action: As the body of Christ, write 3 things you can do to live out Christ this week.

_____
_____
_____
_____
_____
_____
_____
_____
_____
_____

Prayer: Dear Lord, I thank you for your Heavenly Kingdom within me, in the person of Christ and the Holy Spirit. I recognize that my access to your Kingdom is granted because of Jesus Christ. Please, help me to live out this Heavenly Kingdom within me, here on earth.
In Jesus' name, Amen.

Week 25

Authority in Christ

> He said to them, "Because of your little faith. For truly, I say to you, if you have faith like a grain of mustard seed, you will say to this mountain, 'Move from here to there,' and it will move, and nothing will be impossible for you."
> *Matthew 17:20 (ESV)*

Our faith in Christ gives us authority in the Kingdom. In Matthew 28:18-20, Jesus proclaims that He has been given all authority, having defeated death and risen from the grave. By this authority in Christ, we can go into the world and live out the Kingdom of God, having dominion and making disciples of this Kingdom.

The authority we receive through faith in Christ empowers us and places us at God's right hand. This is a place of power, authority, and dominion. This grace came as a result of our righteous status through our faith in Christ.

Our faith in Christ must be expressed in the works we do. If not, it is considered dead and cannot reproduce. Even though it can save our souls, we cannot bear fruit beyond ourselves until we put our faith to work (James 2:17). To reign in this Kingdom, you must start by putting your faith to work. Starting with the little things that bring glory to God (James 2:14-16) increases our authority in the Kingdom of God, even as our mustard seed faith grows.

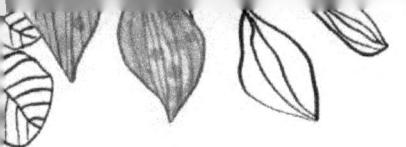

Date_____

Question: What are you believing God for presently, and how can you use that to serve in the Kingdom of God when you receive it?

_____
_____
_____
_____
_____
_____
_____
_____
_____
_____
_____

Action: Write down 3 ways you can put your faith to practice this week.

_____
_____
_____
_____
_____
_____
_____

Prayer: Dear Lord, I thank you for the gift of faith you have given me that saves my soul. Help me to put this faith to practice beyond myself to all those around me.
In Jesus' name, Amen.

Week 26

Living sacrifice

And so, dear brothers and sisters, I plead with you to give your bodies to God because of all He has done for you. Let them be a living and holy sacrifice—the kind He will find acceptable. This is truly the way to worship Him.
Romans 12:1 (NLT)

To be a living sacrifice means we live our daily lives as an offering unto God. Giving ourselves to God for His use. This act of worship starts in our hearts as we follow Christ and obey His teachings. Christ now lives in our hearts in the person of the Holy Spirit and directs us daily. Our ability to follow His instructions and voice as He leads us is how we worship God and bring Him glory.

Following Christ is the true way of offering a sacrifice to God, just as people in the Old Testament did. The pleasing sacrifice is the one that comes from a sincere heart offered by faith (Hebrews 11:4). It requires dying to self and living for God. Sometimes we might put ourselves in an uncomfortable situation in the process of following Christ, but the outcome is life and peace (Romans 8:6).

The more we yield to God in obedience, the more we become transformed to be just like Christ. It is like going to the gym to build up muscles, the process might be painful at first, but once we keep on at it, it becomes a part of us. Christ becomes formed in us, and He takes over to help us be all that God has called us to be.

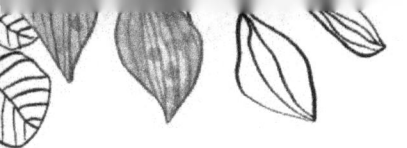
 *Out of Zion* - Journal & Devotional

Date_____

Question: In your present situation, what do you struggle with surrendering to God?

_____
_____
_____
_____
_____
_____
_____
_____
_____
_____
_____

Action: Write down 3 things you can give up for the sake of Christ, as you make this sacrifice to please God.

_____
_____
_____
_____
_____
_____
_____
_____

Prayer: Thank you Jesus for making the greatest sacrifice by laying down your life for me on the cross. Help me God to give this life back to you, totally surrendering myself as a sacrifice to please you. In Jesus' name, Amen.

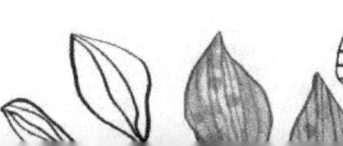

Week 27

Do things well

In His grace, God has given us different gifts for doing certain things well. So, if God has given you the ability to prophesy, speak out with as much faith as God has given you. If your gift is serving others, serve them well. If you are a teacher, teach well. If your gift is to encourage others, be encouraging. If it is giving, give generously. If God has given you leadership ability, take the responsibility seriously. And if you have a gift for showing kindness to others, do it gladly. Don't just pretend to love others. Really love them
Romans 12:6-9(NLT)

Romans 12 says it all. God desires for us to be diligent and strives toward perfection in all we do. When we accomplish things well, it pleases God and brings Him praise, whether at work, school, home, or anywhere else we find ourselves. Remember that you are royalty and represent a perfect Kingdom; therefore, doing things to the best of your ability and constantly striving to be better is one way to rule your world.

We become exemplary leaders that show others the way to our perfect Father as we do things well and God increases us in the process (John 15:2). Being faithful in little opens doors for us to become and have more (Matthew 25:23). This is what it means to arise and shine, and when we do, kings will truly come to the brightness of our rising because we show forth excellence (Isaiah 60:1,3). The key to greatness is in doing things well.

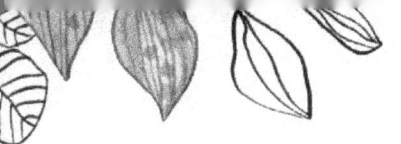

Date_____

Question: In what aspect of your life do you strive for perfection?

_____
_____
_____
_____
_____
_____
_____
_____
_____
_____

Action: Write down 3 ways you can refine your talent, skills, and abilities to become better than you are now.

_____
_____
_____
_____
_____
_____
_____
_____
_____
_____

Prayer: Dear God, thank you for making me a part of your Kingdom. Help me to show forth excellence in all I do as I represent your perfect Kingdom here on earth.
In Jesus' name, Amen.

Week 28

Lead from where you are

> Therefore, go and make disciples of all the nations, baptizing them in the name of the Father and the Son and the Holy Spirit. Teach these new disciples to obey all the commands I have given you. And be sure of this: I am with you always, even to the end of the age."
> *Matthew 28:19-20 (NLT)*

As followers of Jesus Christ, we have been called to leadership. Christ's assignment to us all as we go about our daily lives is to teach and bring people to Him. How can we lead from where we are?

Lend your voice when it is required of you and speak up for justice where there is injustice. Love sincerely, pray for others and show people how to live life by being Christ-like. Use your platforms of influence, which can be your social media platforms or any communication media within your reach, to promote the message of Christ (2 Timothy 4:2, Proverbs 11:14).

We are Christ's ambassadors here on earth, and in the flesh, we are "moving billboards" that advertise Christ. If we conduct our lives in a way that doesn't reflect Christ, we will send the wrong signal and promote a false message about Christ to the world. If we say we are followers of Christ, our lives must reflect who Christ truly is, so we don't lead people astray (1 John 4:20). Remember you are a leader and a priest, destined to rule and reign, and you have the power to lead people toward God or lead them astray.

Date_____

Question: What character of a leader do you possess, and which do you need to work on?

_____
_____
_____
_____
_____
_____
_____
_____
_____
_____
_____
_____

Action: Write down 3 ways you can lead from where you are this week.

_____
_____
_____
_____
_____
_____
_____
_____

Prayer: Thank you God for entrusting me with your work on earth. I recognize that I have been called to lead people to you. Help me God to walk in this consciousness. In Jesus' name, Amen.

Week 29

Lead by serving

> He sat down, called the twelve disciples over to Him, and said, "Whoever wants to be first must take last place and be the servant of everyone else."
> Mark 9:34 (NLT)

It might sound ironic to lead by serving, but Jesus teaches us that whoever wants to become great must lower Himself to be a servant. Serving others builds the right character in us, equipping us to lead right. Since leading requires that we have followers, it means we must have a mindset first to lead ourselves and show others what we are leading them to by being an example. No one has seen God, but they can see God in us with how we conduct our lives. It is the image of God in us they see, that becomes a light to leads them to an even greater light which is God.

One definition of service to humanity is to feed those who are hungry, which relates directly to what Christ asks those who love Him to do. It means taking the place of a shepherd, just as Christ is, and feeding His word, nature, and character to the people He has entrusted into your hands (John 21:17).

We learn to be more like Christ as we serve others and fulfill the obligations given to us by Christ. Leading involves serving all the people Christ entrusts to you, diligently and obediently, just as the shepherd does for the sheep.

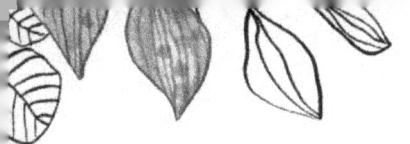

Out of Zion - Journal & Devotional

*Date*_____

Question: Who do you currently have influence over? Your direct report at work, your kids, your siblings, your friends?

_____
_____
_____
_____
_____
_____
_____
_____
_____
_____
_____
_____

Action: Write down 3 ways you can serve them with your skills and talents to glorify God.

_____
_____
_____
_____
_____
_____
_____

Prayer: Thank you God for the gifts you gave to me. I recognize that these gifts (name them) were given to me to serve the people around me. I choose to obey you as you've asked me to feed them. In Jesus' name, Amen.

Week 30

Seek the Kingdom first

Seek the Kingdom of God above all else, and live righteously, and He will give you everything you need.
Matthew 6:33 (NLT)

When Jesus said, "seek first the Kingdom," He meant that we are to set the things of God over the things of the world. Primarily, it indicates that we should seek salvation in God's Kingdom because it is more valuable. Is this to say we should ignore the daily activities that keep our lives going? Definitely not. If we prioritize God's business by seeking His salvation, living in obedience to Him, and sharing the good news of the Kingdom with others, He will take care of our business as He promised.

The Kingdom of God is God's reign on earth, and He wants us to reign with Him. He came to the world as a King to establish His dominion and presence here, laying the foundation with Him being the chief cornerstone (Ephesians 2:20). He also bought for Himself a people, you and I, using His precious blood as the currency of exchange (1 John 1:19).

Now God has entrusted us with the project of building this Kingdom, not leaving it to us but rather being constantly at work in us to do the Kingdom (Philippians 2:13). God plans to finish this work He started at the end when He comes back again in glory to destroy the last enemy which He already defeated at the cross – death (1 Corinthians 15:26).

Date_____

Question: What does it mean to you to seek the Kingdom of God?

_____
_____
_____
_____
_____
_____
_____
_____
_____
_____
_____

Action: Write down 3 Kingdom-focused activities that you can do this week.

_____
_____
_____
_____
_____
_____
_____
_____

Prayer: Dear God, I thank you for establishing your Kingdom here on the earth. I recognize I have been called to build your Kingdom together with Christ as a co-laborer. Oh Lord, please help me to make this my priority. In Jesus' name, Amen.

Week 31

Do it afraid

Trust in the LORD with all your heart; do not depend on your understanding. Seek His will in all you do, and He will show you which path to take.
Proverbs 3:5-6 (NLT)

When God called Abraham to leave his father's house to an unknown destination, Abraham did (Genesis 12:1). Unsure, maybe afraid but still he did, in total obedience, God accounted this as faith (Genesis 15:6). This is the same attitude God wants us to have. The level of our obedience to God tells how much we trust Him. Some things God might ask us to do may seem impossible, daring, or nerve-racking, but we must trust God in the process, knowing that His plans for us are always good and He'll always be there to direct our path.

Doing the things God asks us to do, can sometimes be challenging, but helps to build our faith. By doing so, we overcome the fear and doubt that the enemy brings to keep us from doing the will of the Father. Remember that you have become a part of the body of Christ and have been equipped with special skills and talents to fulfill a unique purpose that has rewards attached to it (Ephesians 2:10).

We must trust God in the process. Even when we are afraid or in doubt, our trust in God must be greater. Great enough to step out of the boat as Peter did (Matthew 14:29). Remember, it's always this - we believe first, then we see (John 11:40).

Out of Zion - Journal & Devotional

Date_____

Question: What fears or doubts do you have about yourself that keeps you from achieving your dreams?

_____
_____
_____
_____
_____
_____
_____
_____
_____
_____

Action: Write down 3 things you can do this week to overcome your fears and doubts.

_____
_____
_____
_____
_____
_____
_____
_____
_____
_____

Prayer: Thank you Lord for the gifts and talents you have given me to serve the world. Help me to put them into use and grant me the grace to trust you even when I feel afraid and unsure. Dear Lord, teach me and lead me as I take this step of faith to do your will.
In Jesus' name, Amen.

Week 32

Write the vision down

And the LORD answered me: "Write the vision; make it plain on tablets, so he may run who reads it.
Habakkuk 2:2 (ESV)

God expects us to take thoughts and carefully write our visions down. In the process, we get clarity and can break them down into smaller goals and actionable plans that are easy to do until we achieve the vision. In Luke 14:28, Jesus tells us, "Suppose one of you wants to build a tower. Won't you first sit down and estimate the cost to see if you have enough money to complete it?"

Creating a vision board and checklist for achieving our big goals provides us with an excellent road map that makes our ambition look possible. Writing down our vision makes us more accountable to ourselves and others, and it serves as a tool for tracking our progress and updating our goals as we progress. Getting an accountability coach that can support us could make the process easier and less terrifying and help us avoid costly mistakes.

Every vision starts as a seed that is nurtured until it grows. Just as with Jesus, who came as the seed of God in Mary's womb, our vision starts as a seed to be nurtured into a mighty tree (Matthew 13:31-32). Just like with a relay race, there should be continuity in our works as we run the race of life and our vision should outlive us. That is why God wants us to write our vision with clarity, so we can easily pass the baton to our successor. Jesus showed this to us with the great commission.

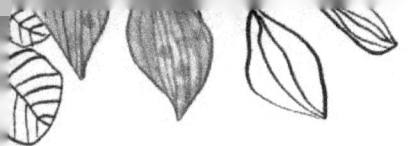

Out of Zion - Journal & Devotional

Date_____

Question: What vision do you have for your life that aligns with advancing the message of Christ? Write them down.

_____
_____
_____
_____
_____
_____
_____
_____

Action: Break down your visions into achievable goals to be accomplished each month/quarter/year.

Months	Goals

Prayer: Dear God, thank you for the vision you have given to me. Help me achieve them as I have written them. In Jesus' name, Amen.

Week 33

Start small

Do not despise these small beginnings, for the LORD rejoices to see the work begin, to see the plumb line in Zerubbabel's hand.
Zechariah 4:10 (NLT)

God loves to see us start; God loves to see our little beginnings when we get the work started, and He is ready to bless those efforts we put in. Like the Kingdom of God, which He describes as a mustard seed that grows into a tree, everything starts as a seed, even the things God does. This means it's okay to start small, ensuring we make deliberate efforts daily towards accomplishing our goals and carefully tracking our progress.

Staying accountable to ourselves is important as God gave us this life to multiply. The expectation in the Kingdom is that we would give an account to God of how we spent this life He gave to us at the end of time (Romans 14:12).

God is pleased when we make little progress and displeased when we do not make any progress at all. The more we desire to multiply that which God has given to us, our talents, our gifts, our skills, the more we receive the power by the help of the Holy Spirit to accomplish them (Philippians 2:13, Deuteronomy 8:18). God who called you, has equipped you with everything you need to accomplish His purpose and plans for your life (2 Timothy 3:17). So go ahead and accomplish your dreams, you've got the power!

Out of Zion - Journal & Devotional

Date_____

Question: What big dreams do you have which require resources within your reach now?

_____
_____
_____
_____
_____
_____
_____
_____
_____
_____

Action: Write down 3 ways you can start achieving them from where you are.

_____
_____
_____
_____
_____
_____
_____
_____
_____

Prayer: Thank you God for the vision you gave to me. I recognize you are pleased when I take a step of faith to begin achieving them. Help me along the way as I begin. In Jesus' name, Amen.

Week 34

Don't stay small

Though thy beginning was small, yet thy latter end should greatly increase.
Job *8:7 (KJV)*

God rejoices when we begin but expects us to increase. John 12:24 tells us, "Unless a kernel of wheat falls to the ground and dies, it remains only a single seed. But if it dies, it produces many seeds." As we offer our gifts and talents to God, trusting Him, He will multiply them. Every branch in Him that bears fruit, He prunes to bear more fruit (John 15:2). And just as He gave up Himself for us, we must also surrender ourselves to Him for the Kingdom's work.

As we begin to walk towards achieving our God-given vision, we must be prepared for the blessings coming our way. Prepare your jars to receive more (2 Kings 4:5). Having a mindset for growth is key. For God can do much more than we would ever dream (Ephesians 3:20).

A growth mindset helps us to think creatively of ways to access resources that may not be within our reach. It also always us to put the right structures in place by setting up a team just as Jesus did by having disciples who served with Him (Luke 6:12-16). With a growth mindset, we would never take no for an answer because we know all things are possible to them that believe (Matthew 19:26), and we would be bold enough to ask for what we need from God and from people who can help us (Matthew 7:7).

Date_____

Question: What big dreams do you have which require resources that are not within your reach now?

_____
_____
_____
_____
_____
_____
_____
_____
_____
_____
_____
_____
_____

Action: Write down 3 ways you can creatively access resources you need to accomplish your plans and put a timeline on when you'll get it done.

_____
_____
_____
_____
_____
_____
_____
_____
_____
_____

Prayer: Thank you God for I know you are a God of all sufficiency and can provide all I need to accomplish the vision you have given to me. I receive grace to accomplish my vision now. In Jesus' name, Amen.

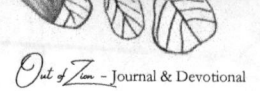

Week 35

Celebrate small wins

Let them praise the LORD for His great love and for the wonderful things he has done for them.
Psalms 107:21 (NLT)

Psalms 35:27 tells us that God delights in our prosperity. If God delights in the small things we accomplish for the Kingdom, we should celebrate ourselves and our small wins. Counting our blessings stirs a heart of gratitude within us and makes us give thanks to God.

The act of thanksgiving to God for the little things we accomplish for His Kingdom provokes His blessings over our lives. Just as with the leper who came back to thank Jesus for healing him and was made whole (Matthew 17:11-19), our sacrifice of praise to God is always pleasing to Him.

Avoid comparing yourself and your accomplishments to others who may have achieved much more. Instead, consider them a source of motivation to lead you to where you want to be. Instead of feeling sorry for yourself, angry, or jealous of what they have accomplished, learn from them, and try to associate yourself with them. Comparison can be dangerous when it fills our hearts with jealousy, so in place of comparison, be confident that you will achieve, even more, work and pray to achieve more, and be content with where you are in your journey. Celebrating your small wins is a way to stir up gratitude and contentment in your heart (1 Timothy 6:6).

Date_____

Question: How much progress have you made with achieving your dreams and visions?
Write down your small wins.

_____
_____
_____
_____
_____
_____
_____
_____
_____
_____
_____

Action: Write down 3 ways you will celebrate these small wins this week.

_____
_____
_____
_____
_____
_____
_____
_____

Prayer: Dear God, thank you for the progress I have made toward accomplishing your plans. Thank you for (mention your small wins). Thank you for giving me the ability to do all things through Christ. In Jesus' name, Amen.

Week 36

Get up and try again

For though the righteous fall seven times, they rise again, but the wicked stumble when calamity strikes.
Proverbs 24:16 (NIV)

Failure is an inevitable aspect of becoming all that God desires you to be. Failure is not the destination; rather, it is a learning point. Learning to pick yourself up after a failed attempt is important in accomplishing your God-given ambitions. It is a way for us to show God that we trust in Him in all situations. There would be adversaries and obstacles that will stand in our way, just as John 16:33 tells us, in this world, we will encounter trouble, but we must be resilient and learn to pick ourselves up after a fall, knowing that Christ has already given us the victory (1 Corinthians 15:57).

Failure could come in the form of rejections, and we must prepare our minds to be accepted by some and rejected by others. Jesus tells us in Mark 6:11, "if any place will not welcome you or listen to you, leave that place and shake the dust off your feet as a testimony against them." Even Jesus Himself was rejected by His people, but this did not stop Him from accomplishing what He came on the earth to do (John 1:11).

Accept failure and rejection as part of the process of becoming all that God wants you to be. Don't let it prevent you from moving forward, rather learn from it and use it as your springboard to getting ahead.

 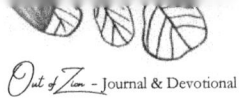

*Date*_____

Question: What have you failed at? List them

_____
_____
_____
_____
_____
_____
_____
_____
_____
_____
_____

Action: Write down 3 ways you can use your failure as a springboard to accomplish your God-given plans.

_____
_____
_____
_____
_____
_____
_____
_____

Prayer: Thank you God for all the times I have failed and experienced rejection. Help me to learn from these experiences as you use them as a springboard to getting me to where you want me to be. In Jesus' name, Amen.

Week 37

Drink up

Like newborn babies, you must crave pure spiritual milk so that you will grow into a full experience of salvation. Cry out for this nourishment.
1 Peter 2:2 (NLT)

To operate in God's Kingdom, where we rule, reign, and exercise dominion on the earth, we must attain spiritual maturity. This is because feeding a flock requires giving from what we have within us. You cannot pour from an empty cup or give what you don't have. It is important that you drink up the nourishment of God's word, so you can be enriched to feed and nurture others.

Jesus is the water of life which we drink of and never thirst again, but rather this water becomes in us a fountain of water springing up to eternal life (John 4:14). It is this fountain that flows out from our belly as rivers of living water that others around us can drink of (John 7:37). So, we must fill ourselves with God's word until it overflows.

As we operate in this Kingdom and start giving ourselves to the service of God, the virtue within us which gets used up must be replenished (Luke 8:46). The water of God's word within us is meant to keep flowing like a river, and we must ensure we stay connected to the source and keep abiding in the vine which is God and the word of God (John 15:4). We do this by praying, meditating and obeying the word as we operate in the Kingdom of God.

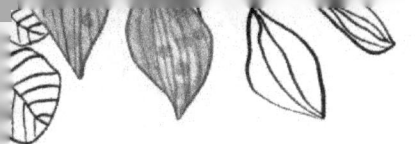

Date_____

Question: What areas of your spiritual life do you need to develop?

_____
_____
_____
_____
_____
_____
_____
_____
_____
_____
_____
_____

Action: Write down 3 ways you would drink up to build up those areas.

_____
_____
_____
_____
_____
_____
_____
_____
_____
_____

Prayer: Dear God, I thank you for your word that nourishes me and makes me grow in you. Help me to stay connected to you as I operate in your Kingdom and have dominion on the earth. In Jesus' name, Amen.

Week 38

Learn something new

Intelligent people are always ready to learn. Their ears are open for knowledge.
Proverbs 18:15 (NLT)

Proverbs 18:15 tells us we are wise and intelligent when we seek to learn something new often. The more we know, the more we can increase our level of influence and gain approval (2 Timothy 2:15). God wants us to add more knowledge to what we currently have, so we can speak with boldness and confidence and contribute to diverse conversations. This confidence in knowledge is one way we can exercise and increase our influence.

John 14:26 remind us that we have an advocate in the person of the Holy Spirit, whom the Father has sent to us to teach us all things, and He teaches us what we need to know at every point in time, giving us this knowledge according to our unique purpose and calling to accomplish what He wants us to for that time and season.

Increasing in knowledge makes us increase in power – this power goes beyond physical strength to speak of dominion, rulership, and authority (Proverbs 24:5). Knowledge from God also brings deliverance from darkness because true knowledge is light (Proverbs 11:9, John 8:32) and as we receive light and increase in our influence, we attract kings and nations that come to us bringing their wealth and riches to serve us (Isaiah 60:3, Proverbs 24:4).

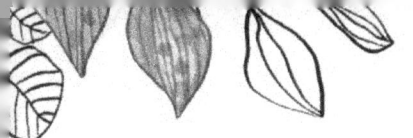
 Journal & Devotional

Date_____

Question: What aspects of your gifts and talents do you need more knowledge on to become skillful at?

_____
_____
_____
_____
_____
_____
_____
_____
_____

Action: Write down 3 new things you will learn this week to contribute to developing your gifts and talents.

_____
_____
_____
_____
_____
_____
_____

Prayer: Thank you Lord for your Holy Spirit that is always with me to teach me. I open my heart to receive wisdom and knowledge as I develop the gifts and talents you gave to me and the grace to impact a generation.
In Jesus' name, Amen.

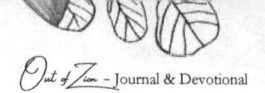

Week 39

Make God's word a habit

> But they delight in the law of the LORD, meditating on it day and night. They are like trees planted along the riverbank, bearing fruit each season. Their leaves never wither, and they prosper in all they do.
> *Psalms 1:2-3 (NLT)*

As we operate in God's Kingdom, we must prioritize the things of God's Kingdom over every activity in our daily lives. This can happen when we make reading God's word a habit. New habits, like any other, are developed by doing things repeatedly. God wants us to be skillful in His word (2 Timothy 2:15). This is the operating manual of the Kingdom of God and is also our weapon and staff of authority (Ephesians 6:17).

Life's activity sometimes interferes with our bible study time, especially in this social media age. A more intentional and purposeful effort is required. Understanding that the strategy of the devil is to bring distractions and to steal God's word which is your power, from you (Romans 1:16).

It only takes days to form a habit, and once that habit is formed, we naturally keep maintaining it, although the initial stage requires constant feeding and nurturing. Remember that reading God's word is a good habit that helps you bear fruit and prosper (Psalms 1:2), so forming this habit is worth every penny of your time.

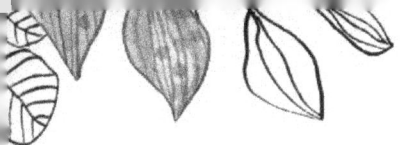

*Date*_____

Question: What new habits do you need to form to become a master of your skill?

_____
_____
_____
_____
_____
_____
_____
_____
_____
_____
_____
_____

Action: Write down 3 ways you can start developing these new habits.

_____
_____
_____
_____
_____
_____
_____
_____
_____
_____

Prayer: Heavenly Father, I thank you for your word that bears fruit in me as I make a habit to meditate daily on it. Help me God to stay consistent in reading and studying your word. In Jesus' name, Amen.

Week 40

Be wise

For the LORD gives wisdom; from His mouth come knowledge and understanding.
Proverbs 2:16 (NIV)

Wisdom comes from God, and we receive this wisdom as we walk with God, reading His word and following Christ. It's important to be wise in this world because the days are evil, and as we walk in wisdom, we redeem the time, which is a gift from God (Ephesians 5:15-16). How do you spend this gift of time which God has given to you? How we spend our time shows how wise we are.

Ecclesiastes 2:26 tells us, "To the person who pleases Him, God gives wisdom, knowledge, and happiness, but to the sinner, He gives the task of gathering and storing up wealth to hand it over to the one who pleases God. This too is meaningless, a chasing after the wind." This scripture explains that pleasing God by being obedient to Him; is indeed a wise thing to do.

The Kingdom belongs to the wise, which is why the foolish virgins could not enter the Kingdom of God (Matthew 25:10). God needs wise people to redeem the lost, and Colossians 4:5-6 teaches us how to act wisely as representatives of the Kingdom of God here on earth. It tells us to be wise in the way we act toward outsiders and make the most of every opportunity as we let our conversations always be full of grace and seasoned with words of wisdom, so we know how to answer everyone.

Out of Zion - Journal & Devotional

Date_____

Question: What has God asked you to do lately?

_____
_____
_____
_____
_____
_____
_____
_____
_____
_____
_____
_____

Action: Write down 3 things you will start doing to please God so you can increase in wisdom.

_____
_____
_____
_____
_____
_____
_____
_____
_____
_____

Prayer: Dear Lord, I thank you for the gift of faith you have given me that saves my soul. Help me to be wise and put this faith to work beyond myself to all those around me. In Jesus' name, Amen.

Week 41

Find your voice

It is written: "I believed; therefore, I have spoken." Since we have that same spirit of faith, we also believe and therefore speak
2 Corinthians 4:13 (NIV)

Our faith in Christ stirs in us a faith that makes us speak. When your heart is so full of the word of God, your mouth becomes an outlet for that overflow (Ecclesiastes 11:3). God wants us to be full of His word. The power in your voice is measured by the quality of God's word in you, as you let the Holy Spirit have His way in you (Zechariah 4:6).

The power of your voice is in the voice of God, and you find God's voice in His word. In the Kingdom of God, the angels obey the command of God, and when we speak the word of God, we take on the voice of God (Psalms 103:20). This is the voice of power and authority (Hebrews 4:12). That is why we must always come before God in the person of Jesus Christ whom we have become, coming in His name.

As we operate in the Kingdom of God, we must give ourselves to the Gospel's message, letting our voice become the voice of Christ to bring the message of truth to the lost sheep. In your heart is a treasure filled with the goodness of God, His word, your experiences, and your encounters with who God is. Let this treasure out through the words you speak, speaking grace and life to those around you (2 Corinthians 4:7).

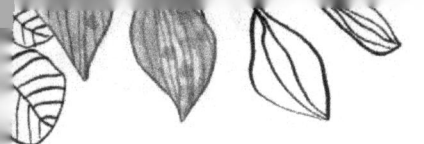

Out of Zion - Journal & Devotional

Date_____

Question: What in the world seem disturbing to you that you feel you can do something about?

_____
_____
_____
_____
_____
_____
_____
_____
_____
_____
_____

Action: Write down 3 ways you can lend your voice to the situations around you

_____
_____
_____
_____
_____
_____
_____
_____
_____
_____

Prayer: Oh Lord, I thank you for the gift of your voice in me. I choose to give your voice expressions through my lips, letting your good treasures in me out through my lips. Holy Spirit, fill me up until I overflow.
In Jesus' name, Amen.

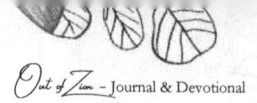

Week 42

Thrive

Those that be planted in the house of the LORD shall flourish in the courts of our God.
Psalms 92:13-14 (KJV)

You are the planting of the Lord, and God has placed you in this Kingdom to flourish (Isaiah 61:3). To thrive and flourish, you must stay rooted in the vine – Christ. In Christ, who is the water of life, you receive all the nourishment to flourish and bear fruit (Psalm 1:3). Then you become an oak of righteousness that flourishes like the palm tree planted by the streams of water (Psalms 92:12)

We must ensure we stay connected to the vine in every area of our lives to experience an all-around flourishing life. We do this by reading and meditating on the word of God and obeying God in everything we do, as the Holy Spirit prompts us.

The evidence of our faith is seen as we thrive in the Kingdom of God, bearing fruits in the form of good works (James 2:14). For faith without works is dead and the good work we produce is what God ordained before time began that we should walk in (Ephesians 2:10). As we get planted in Christ, we start bearing fruits, and the seeds of these fruits continuously produce more fruits with Christ pruning us (2 Corinthians 9:10, John 15:2). This is what brings glory to God (Matthew 5:16).

Date_____

Question: How can the evidence of your faith be seen through your works?

_____
_____
_____
_____
_____
_____
_____
_____
_____
_____
_____
_____

Action: Write down 3 ways you can put your skills and talent to work so you can glorify God.

_____
_____
_____
_____
_____
_____
_____
_____
_____
_____
_____

Prayer: Thank you God for planting me in your house and connecting me to Christ who is the vine. I receive the water of life to flourish in the vine where I have been planted by you. In Jesus' name, Amen.

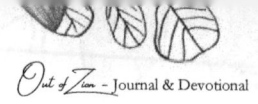

Week 43

Tares or wheat

Another parable put He forth unto them, saying, The Kingdom of heaven is likened unto a man which sowed good seed in his field: But while men slept, his enemy came and sowed tares among the wheat, and went his way. But when the blade was sprung up and brought forth fruit, then appeared the tares also.
Matthew 13:24-26 (KJV)

There are two sets of people producing fruits on the earth. Some produce wheat which is a good crop planted by God, while some produce tares planted by the enemy that looks somewhat like wheat but is nothing like it. These tares are weeds planted by the enemy to attack our faith or hinder our growth. They come in different forms to distract us, compete with us, or make us terrified or insecure.

We must do a self-check on ourselves often to ensure we are not producing tares which are the fruit of unrighteousness and works of the flesh like anger, bitterness, jealousy, and idolatry (Galatians 5:19). Rather, we must continuously allow the Holy Spirit to produce in us wheat which are fruits of righteousness and of the Spirit like love, joy, peace, patience, and kindness (Galatians 5:22).

The fruit we bear depends on the word we choose to nurture in our hearts. We must ensure we are nurturing the word of God in our hearts and not the words of the enemy.

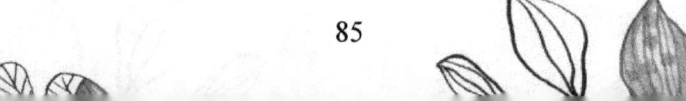

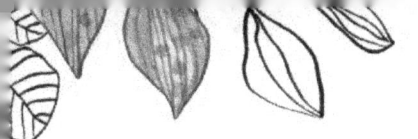

Out of Zion - Journal & Devotional

Date_____

Question: What kind of fruit are you producing? Name them and identify any fruit you want more of.

_____
_____
_____
_____
_____
_____
_____
_____
_____
_____
_____
_____

Action: Write down 3 ways you can nurture the word of God in your heart to produce more fruit.

_____
_____
_____
_____
_____
_____
_____
_____

Prayer: Almighty Father, I praise and thank you for your words in my heart. I choose to nurture these words by meditating, praying, and doing them so I can produce fruits of righteousness that are pleasing to you. Help me to give more time to your word that strengthens my faith in you. In Jesus' name, Amen.

Week 44

No to slothfulness

And we desire each one of you to show the same earnestness to have the full assurance of hope until the end, so that you may not be sluggish, but imitators of those who through faith and patience inherit the promises.
Hebrews 6:11-12 (ESV)

Slothfulness toward God and the Kingdom can keep us from reaching our full potential and as a result, from being all that God intends for us to be. There are many treasures within you, and they require your diligence and commitment to first discover them, then develop them until they become skills, and then you multiply them.

God deposited these treasures in the earth by planting them as seeds in earthen vessels - you and I (2 Corinthians 4:7), so we can reproduce till they fill and replenish the earth with a rich glorious inheritance (Ephesians 1:18).

So, with diligence, let us work in this vineyard with a multiplication consciousness. Keeping track of our progress as we multiply so we can be accountable to the One who has called us, knowing that the King requires this of us. So that at His return, He shall find faith in us that produced good works (Luke 18:8) and we will hear just as in Matthew 25:23-30, "well done, good and trustworthy servant" rather than, "throw this good-for-nothing, evil and lazy slave into the outer darkness."

Date_____

Question: What hidden treasures do you have within you in the form of gifts and talents?

_____
_____
_____
_____
_____
_____
_____
_____
_____
_____

Action: Write down 3 things you will do to develop them into a skill or 3 ways you will put them to use to multiply them if you are already skillful at them.

_____
_____
_____
_____
_____
_____
_____

Prayer: Thank you God for the treasures you have put inside of me. I choose to be diligent and dedicated to discovering them, developing them, and multiplying them to give you all the glory. In Jesus' name, Amen.

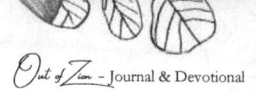

Week 45

Be a doer of the word

But don't just listen to God's word. You must do what it says. Otherwise, you are only fooling yourselves.
James 1:22 (NLT)

The Word of God is a viable seed, quick and alive (Hebrews 4:12), but the ground it is planted in determines if it will grow and the rate at which it will multiply (Matthew 13:4-8).

Just as with every seed, a wise gardener knows they require care and nurturing to grow. Likewise, with God's Word, we must prepare the ground and lay the foundation that is required of us to have dominion. Setting the foundation requires that when we come across a revelation in God's Word, we meditate on it by searching scriptures that relate to it (John 5:39). These connecting scriptures become witnesses to the Word and faith in our hearts, bringing light and insight to us and forming a solid foundation that cannot be moved (Mathew 13:23). It is with this understanding that we then pray and praise, speaking the Word - watering it and giving it life so it can take further root in us, bearing fruit – the fruit of the Spirit seen in our character as we transform. This is the good work our faith produces (2 Corinthians 13:1, Galatians 5:22-23).

This is what makes us wise, blessed, and fruitful, holding on to a faith with evidence that cannot be moved or shaken, a kind of faith that is welcomed in God's unshakable Kingdom (Matthew 7:24, Hebrews 12:27).

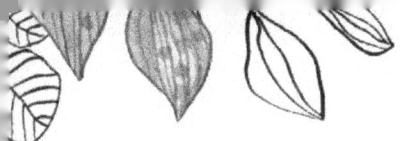

Date_____

Question: What part of God's word do you struggle with believing and/or doing?

_____
_____
_____
_____
_____
_____
_____
_____
_____
_____
_____
_____

Action: Find 3 scriptures that speak to the areas where you struggle and meditate on them this week.

_____
_____
_____
_____
_____
_____
_____
_____
_____

Prayer: Dear God, I recognize that your word is active and powerful. I make a commitment to prepare the ground of my heart through diligent studying of your word, so it can take root in me and bear fruit to please you, as I become a doer of your word. In Jesus' name, Amen.

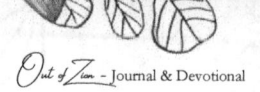

Week 46

Work that is fireproof

But on judgment day, fire will reveal what kind of work each builder has done. The fire will show if a person's work has any value.
1 Corinthians 3:11-13 (NLT)

As we build upon Christ, we must ensure the quality of our work is durable with eternal value. The Bible clarifies to us that there are works of the flesh and the manifestation of the Spirit. The defining factor between these two is relative to the ruling factor. So, what rules over you determines the type of work you produce.

The work of the flesh is manifested in the Kingdom of darkness, where the devil rules over people who do not know Christ, the light of the world, and those who have not fully come to understand the truth of Christ's message that sets free and brings light. They respond to the things that rule the flesh and can only yield unrighteous fruit. This kind of fruit cannot stand the fire (Galatians 5:19-21).

But those in Christ have received a treasure which is the Kingdom of God that cannot be consumed by fire but instead is refined to its best version. So that our light affliction which is but for a moment can work for us, a far more exceeding and eternal weight of glory. We diligently nurture the faith in our hearts by receiving light through God's word that makes us produce good works. This kind of work is fireproof and with eternal value (Galatians 5:22-24, 1 Corinthians 12:6-11).

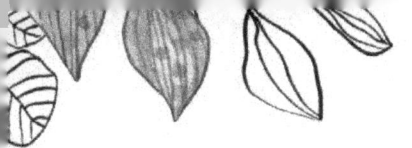

Date_____

Question: In what areas of your life do you struggle with bearing the fruit of the spirit and what unrighteous fruit do you bear?

_____
_____
_____
_____
_____
_____
_____
_____
_____

Action: Write down 3 things you can do this week to allow the Holy Spirit to bear fruit in you.

_____
_____
_____
_____
_____
_____
_____
_____

Prayer: Thank you God for the gift of the Holy Spirit that brings light and rules over me, bearing fruit that is fireproof and eternal. I choose to give the Holy Spirit room to bear more fruit in me as I surrender myself to obeying and pleasing you. In Jesus' name, Amen.

Week 47

We are the body

> Now you are the body of Christ, and each one of you is a part of it.
> *1 Corinthians 12:27 (NIV)*

Each one of us is a part of the body of Christ, baptized by one Spirit to form one body, united for the Kingdom with Christ being the head. We have been given the ministry of reconciliation, so we operate on the earth as God's ambassadors to reconcile the world to God (2 Corinthians 5:18-20).

Each part of God's body has been equipped with special gifts and abilities to work effectively within different departments in God's Kingdom so that in collaboration, we can all achieve God's purpose for the earth. In God's Kingdom, teamwork also makes the dream work, and love is what unites and makes us stronger to achieve the purpose to which we have been called (1 Corinthians 12:31).

We are on a mission to take away the enmity by bringing reconciliation between God and non-believers, so we must stay reconciled to each other in the Kingdom. We do not compete, hate or bring down members of the body of Christ, but rather we support, encourage, and love all those who are part of the body of Christ as we work together to achieve God's mission for the earth (2 Corinthians 5:14-15, Galatians 6:10). Creating for Him a Kingdom with systems and a display of skills, talents and working faith from different members of the body of Christ, that He would some day come to possess.

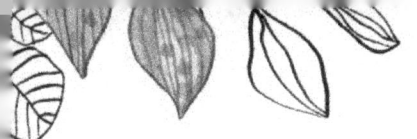

Date_____

Question: In what way do you contribute to the body of Christ? What department do you function in?

_____
_____
_____
_____
_____
_____
_____
_____
_____
_____
_____
_____

Action: Write down 3 ways you can show love and support those who are part of the body of Christ.

_____
_____
_____
_____
_____
_____
_____
_____

Prayer: Thank you Lord for the gift of your body – Christ and your spirit that makes us one together with Christ. Show me where you have placed me in your body to function and help me to support and show love to those who are part of this body. In Jesus' name, Amen.

Week 48

In deeds and in truth

Dear children, let us not love with words or speech but with actions and in truth.
1 John 3:18 (NIV)

God has called us to love. Love is the driving force in the Kingdom of God that propels us to do the work of the Kingdom. We can have dominion over the earth and carry out our God-given assignments when we encounter the love of God that makes us love Him in return and genuinely love others. Love made Christ come to the earth to lay down His life, and love should make us lay down our lives for others (1 John 3:16).

Receiving the love of God in our hearts is where it all begins. Then we can love God, ourselves, and others. You cannot give what you don't have, so you must receive love from God to be able to give genuine love (1 John 4:19).

Our love for God must transcend beyond words into actions. So, we do the work of the Kingdom because we genuinely love God. In the same way, we must also love people around us beyond what we say to them. This is one way we can express the faith in our heart that produces good works (Titus 2:14). It is our love in action that brings glory and praise to God. Let that light of Jesus in you shine before all to see through your act of love. This is how God expects us to operate in the Kingdom of God.

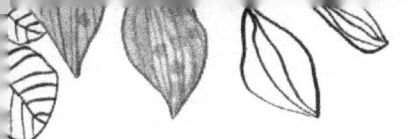
 *Out of Zion* – Journal & Devotional

Date_____

Question: In what ways have you encountered the love of God?

_____
_____
_____
_____
_____
_____
_____
_____
_____
_____
_____
_____

Action: Write down 3 ways you can express the love of God within you to those around you.

_____
_____
_____
_____
_____
_____
_____
_____

Prayer: Thank you God for your love in my heart. Help me to give this love to those around me as I put them into action, loving in deeds and in truth to give you the praise. In Jesus' name, Amen.

Week 49

Designed to multiply

As for you, be fruitful and increase in number; multiply on the earth and increase upon it."
Genesis 9:7 (NIV)

God designed the earth for multiplication, and He designed man to be the proprietor of the earth to multiply. Genesis 2:5 shows us a pattern where God sends water on the earth and forms man to till the ground so it could bring forth and multiply. In the same way, God sends the rain on the earth, He also sends His Word, planting them as seeds in our hearts, in earthen vessels so that we can multiply (Isaiah 55:10-11).

We must put in the work to till this ground and allow the seed of God's word to be planted in us, even as we stay attached to the water of life – Jesus, and we receive all we need to bring forth a harvest unto God (2 Corinthians 4:7).

You were designed to multiply, and God wants you to. Our heart is the ground where God plants His seeds, but He requires us to be good grounds for His word to bring forth fruit. How we receive and understand God's word tells if our hearts are 'good grounds' or not. The more we study the word, the more we gain understanding as we receive light. This is the ground-tilling process that requires us to put in the work and as we do, we make our hearts good grounds to receive the seed of God's word for multiplication (Matthew 13:18-23). We exercise dominion as we multiply God's word on the earth.

Date_____

Question: What seed has God planted in your heart for multiplication?

_____
_____
_____
_____
_____
_____
_____
_____
_____
_____
_____
_____

Action: Write down 3 actions you will take this week to prepare your heart to multiply God's word that is planted in your heart.

_____
_____
_____
_____
_____
_____
_____

Prayer: Heavenly Father, I thank you for the gift of faith you have given to me that saves my soul. Help me to put this faith to work beyond myself to all those around me. In Jesus' name, Amen.

Week 50

The harvest is ready

Don't you have a saying, 'It's still four months until harvest'? I tell you, open your eyes and look at the fields! They are ripe for harvest. Even now the one who reaps draws a wage and harvests a crop for eternal life, so that the Sower and the reaper may be glad together.
John 4:35-36 (NIV)

There is a reward for working in God's Kingdom. The reward we receive is the joy of eternal life for the saved souls brought into the Kingdom of God (Romans 6:23, Luke 15:10). We work in His vineyard to harvest a Kingdom and people for our God.

We are in union with one another as the body of Christ, performing different roles as God requires of us. He plants His word as seeds in the hearts of people and at some point, God could use us as the tool for planting and at other times, the tool for watering (1 Corinthians 3:6). In all, God is the one who provides the seed and makes it grow (2 Corinthians 9:10). So, all we are is a tool in the hand of God, ready to be used (Ephesians 2:10).

We must always act in obedience to God and allow Him to use us for His glory. We were created for God's glory, and this is the only way we can experience the fullness of God and become all that God wants us to be. As we do, we reap a harvest of righteousness – which is the Kingdom of God (2 Corinthians 9:10, Romans 14:17). God takes us to new heights of dominion, power, and authority in His Kingdom.

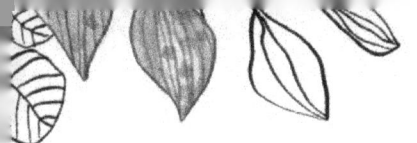

Date_____

Question: How can you position yourself in God's vineyard to reap the harvest of the seed He has sown?

_____
_____
_____
_____
_____
_____
_____
_____
_____
_____
_____

Action: Write down 3 ways you can allow God to use you for His will.

_____
_____
_____
_____
_____
_____
_____
_____

Prayer: Dear Lord, I thank you for planting the seed and placing me in your vineyard to reap this bountiful harvest. I receive insight to see the harvest and the grace to reap a harvest for the Kingdom of God.
In Jesus' name, Amen.

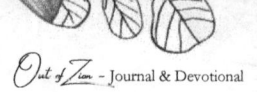

Week 51

This is eternal life

Now, this is eternal life: that they know you, the only true God, and Jesus Christ, whom you have sent.
John 17:3 (NIV)

We must know that we are on a journey to discovering and knowing God intimately. The more of God we know, the more we are transformed to be like Him. We drink of a kind of water that becomes a well in us, springing up to eternal life, we receive this life as we know Christ who is eternal life (John 14:6, 4:14).

Sometimes we get too busy to spend quality time with God. God understands our needs as humans, but He requires us to take a step closer to Him every day to know Him better. God desires that our encounter with Him be as personal and intimate as possible because He has made each of us uniquely different for a specific purpose. As we start fulfilling our purpose, we get on a journey of discovering God on a personal level; beyond the bible we read, then our lives become an epistle others may read and be inspired by, as they come to learn about God through us.

In the process of working with God, we get to discover who He is and encounter Him in ways that are unique to our purpose. We are filled with the knowledge of God in the person of Jesus Christ, who is eternal life (John 14:6) and this knowledge is revealed through us by faith to those around us, transcending generations to eternity (Habakkuk 2:14, 2 Corinthians 3:18, Hebrews 11:4).

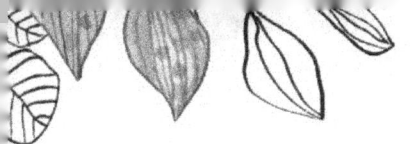
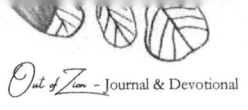

Out of Zion – Journal & Devotional

Date_____

Question: If you were to write your life as an epistle for others to read and be inspired to know God more, what would you write?

_____
_____
_____
_____
_____
_____
_____
_____
_____
_____
_____
_____

Action: Write down 3 ways you can use your unique gifts and talents in God's Kingdom to continue the journey to knowing God intimately.

_____
_____
_____
_____
_____
_____
_____
_____
_____

Prayer: Thank you God for the gift of faith you have given me that saves my soul. Help me to put this faith to work beyond myself to all those around me.
In Jesus' name, Amen.

Week 52

Go for gold, finish strong

I have fought the good fight, I have finished the race, and I have kept the faith. Now there is in store for me the crown of righteousness, which the Lord, the righteous Judge, will award to me on that day—and not only to me but also to all who have longed for His appearing.
2 Timothy 4:7-8 (NIV)

As we take on our kingly place in God's Kingdom, doing the work of the Kingdom as God has called us to, we must ensure we finish strong. A crown of eternal life and righteousness awaits us at the end. We receive our heavenly possessions, a glorious incorruptible body designed to reign with Christ on the earth forever. (Philippians 3:20-21)

While we wait for this day to come, let us continue doing the works of God's Kingdom in faith, and be firm in God, going for gold and never accepting defeat. Remember that while we are on the earth to bring the knowledge of truth to the lost, we are on the battleground where we must constantly fight the good fight of faith, knowing what to answer to everyone asking about our hope (1 peter 3:15), tearing down every lie and demolishing every argument that sets itself up against God's Word. We take every thought captive and bring them to the obedience of Christ (2 Corinthians 10:5).

God is with you, and with God, you can do all things (Matthew 28:20, Philippians 4:13). So, go for gold and finish strong!!!

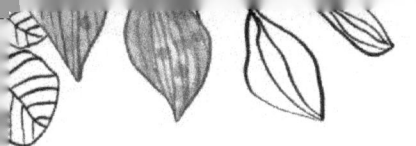

Date_____

Question: How are you keeping the faith and preserving the message of truth while you await your crown?

_____
_____
_____
_____
_____
_____
_____
_____
_____
_____
_____
_____
_____

Action: Write down 3 things you will do this week to build your faith in God.

_____
_____
_____
_____
_____
_____
_____
_____
_____

Prayer: Thank you God for the gift of faith you have given to me that makes me function in this Kingdom. Help me to continue to fight the good fight of faith as I await your glorious crown. In Jesus' name, Amen.

Conclusion

The journey and process of becoming all that God wants you to be starts with knowing who you are, whose you are and where you have been brought to.

1 Peter 2:9 tells who you are:
- You are royalty – a royal priesthood
- A chosen generation
- God's special people
- Seated in heavenly places
- Brought to mount Zion, the city of our God to proclaim the praise of God, who has brought you from the kingdom of darkness to the Kingdom of light in Christ.

It is no mistake that you are referred to as more than one person because in you is a nation waiting to be birthed. The whole world both visible and invisible awaits your manifestation (Romans 8:19).

If you would be so gracious and kind, please introduce yourself:

"I am a functional part of the body of Christ, making expressions on the earth and building for our God, an unshakable Kingdom that will someday be my inheritance. I am crowned and royalty, a priest unto our God, the Father's pride, born of the Spirit of God with the DNA of Christ. A kingmaker and a reigning king whom Christ – the King of kings reigns over."

Further reading:

- 2 Timothy 2:12
- Revelation 1:6
- Revelation 5:10
- Matthew 28:19-20
- Luke 22:28-30
- Matthew 25:34
- Luke 12:32
- Acts 20:32
- 1 Peter 1:3-5

A Psalm of triumph sung by the saints of God as heard in the Author's vision.

"Out of Zion,
Hear the voice of the triumph sing,
Hallelujah! To the King!"

Discover Your Purpose Trivia Quiz

If you had a superpower, what would it be and what would you do with it?

_____
_____
_____
_____
_____
_____
_____
_____
_____
_____
_____

If you were left on an island alone for 1 year, what would you do to survive?

_____
_____
_____
_____
_____
_____
_____
_____
_____
_____
_____

Discover Your Purpose Trivia Quiz

If you were left alone with no one watching, how would you give God your highest praise?

_____
_____
_____
_____
_____
_____
_____
_____
_____
_____
_____

What is the most daring thing you can do for God?

_____
_____
_____
_____
_____
_____
_____
_____
_____
_____
_____
_____

Discover Your Purpose Trivia Quiz

What can you do for free for people that also makes you happy?

_____
_____
_____
_____
_____
_____
_____
_____
_____
_____

If you did not have to work for the rest of your life because you got all the money in the world that you need, what would you do with your life?

_____
_____
_____
_____
_____
_____
_____
_____
_____
_____
_____
_____

Long-Term Vision Planner

What is your long-term vision and how does this relate to your God-given purpose and assignment?

_____
_____
_____
_____
_____
_____
_____
_____
_____
_____
_____
_____
_____
_____
_____
_____
_____
_____
_____
_____
_____
_____
_____
_____
_____
_____

And the LORD answered me: "Write the vision; make it plain on tablets, so he may run who reads it. – Habakkuk 2:2 (ESV)

Vision Planner – 6 months

In the next 6 months, what do you plan to achieve toward reaching your long-term vision?

_____
_____
_____
_____
_____
_____
_____
_____
_____
_____
_____
_____
_____
_____
_____
_____
_____
_____
_____
_____
_____
_____
_____
_____
_____
_____
_____

And the LORD answered me: "Write the vision; make it plain on tablets, so he may run who reads it. – Habakkuk 2:2 (ESV)

Vision Planner – Year 1

By year 1, what do you plan to achieve toward reaching your long-term vision?

___
___
___
___
___
___
___
___
___
___
___
___
___
___
___
___
___
___
___
___
___
___
___
___
___
___

And the LORD answered me: "Write the vision; make it plain on tablets, so he may run who reads it. – Habakkuk 2:2 (ESV)

Vision Planner – Year 2

By year 2, what do you plan to achieve toward reaching your long-term vision?

_____
_____
_____
_____
_____
_____
_____
_____
_____
_____
_____
_____
_____
_____
_____
_____
_____
_____
_____
_____
_____
_____
_____
_____
_____
_____

And the LORD answered me: "Write the vision; make it plain on tablets, so he may run who reads it. – Habakkuk 2:2 (ESV)

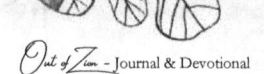

Vision Planner – Year 3

By year 3, what do you plan to achieve toward reaching your long-term vision?

_____
_____
_____
_____
_____
_____
_____
_____
_____
_____
_____
_____
_____
_____
_____
_____
_____
_____
_____
_____
_____
_____
_____
_____
_____
_____
_____

And the LORD answered me: "Write the vision; make it plain on tablets, so he may run who reads it. – Habakkuk 2:2 (ESV)

Vision Planner – Year 4

By year 4, what do you plan to achieve toward reaching your long-term vision?

_____
_____
_____
_____
_____
_____
_____
_____
_____
_____
_____
_____
_____
_____
_____
_____
_____
_____
_____
_____
_____
_____
_____
_____
_____
_____

And the LORD answered me: "Write the vision; make it plain on tablets, so he may run who reads it. – Habakkuk 2:2 (ESV)

 *Out of Zion* – Journal & Devotional

Vision Planner – Year 5

By year 5, what do you plan to achieve toward reaching your long-term vision?

_____
_____
_____
_____
_____
_____
_____
_____
_____
_____
_____
_____
_____
_____
_____
_____
_____
_____
_____
_____
_____
_____
_____
_____
_____
_____

And the LORD answered me: "Write the vision; make it plain on tablets, so he may run who reads it. – Habakkuk 2:2 (ESV)

Notes & Reflections

I will go before thee, and make the crooked places straight: I will break in pieces the gates of brass, and cut in sunder the bars of iron – Isaiah 45:2 (KJV)

Notes & Reflections

Only ask, and I will give you the nations as your inheritance, the whole earth as your possession – Psalms 2:8 (NLT)

Notes & Reflections

So, this is what the Sovereign LORD says: "See, I lay a stone in Zion, a tested stone, a precious cornerstone for a sure foundation; the one who relies on it will never be stricken with panic. – Isaiah 28:16 (NIV)

Notes & Reflections

Then I looked, and there before me was the Lamb, standing on Mount Zion, and with Him 144,000 who had His name and His Father's name written on their foreheads. — Revelation 14:1 (NIV)

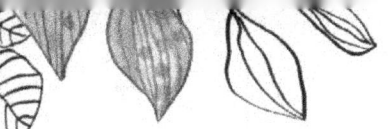 

Notes & Reflections

And they sang a new song before the throne and before the four living creatures and the elders. No one could learn the song except the 144,000 who had been redeemed from the earth. — Revelation 14:3 (NIV)

Notes & Reflections

Rejoice greatly, O daughter of Zion! Shout aloud, O daughter of Jerusalem! Behold, your king is coming to you; righteous and having salvation is He, humble and mounted on a donkey, on a colt, the foal of a donkey. – Zechariah 9:9 (ESV)

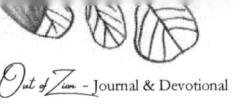

Notes & Reflections

To the one who is victorious, I will give the right to sit with me on my throne, just as I was victorious and sat down with my Father on His throne. – Revelation 3:21 (NIV)

About the Author

Anthonia Udemeh is an artist and songwriter, known professionally as Thonia. She is a published author with a passion for God, people, and storytelling. Thonia's rich and warm vocal delivery provides the backbone for her original songs. She released her debut single, "Out of Zion" in November 2022.

Thonia's ministry is drawn towards women and children, as she provides mentoring and support to them through her artistic and ministerial work. She created the Out of Zion Tribe – a community for women who desire to take their place of dominion in the Kingdom of God and currently volunteers as a spiritual support with YouVersion where she lends herself to praying for those in need. She is the founder of Kids of God - an organization created to bring kids to the saving knowledge of Jesus Christ through music and written works of art that bring them closer to God.

Thonia's ministry started in 2019 after an encounter she had with God as He revealed the end time to her in a revelation. This encounter changed the trajectory of her life as she gained a sense of urgency for the work of the Kingdom to save the souls of those perishing and to bring the knowledge of truth to all, through her songs, books, and ministerial work.

Scan the QR code or visit https://thonia.start.page to learn more about the Author:

www.ingramcontent.com/pod-product-compliance
Lightning Source LLC
Chambersburg PA
CBHW051849160426
43209CB00006B/1227